The Turtle Room

The Turtle Room

Essays

Rosemary Kennevan-Ashbaugh

Library of Congress Control Number		2012902912
ISBN:	Softcover	978-1-4691-5838-9
	Ebook	978-1-4691-5839-6

This book was printed in the United States of America.

To order additional copies of this book, contact:
Xlibris Corporation
1-888-795-4274
www.Xlibris.com
Orders@xlibris.com
111136

Contents

Dedication

You'll never plow a field by turning it over in your mind.

Irish Wisdom

Thanks Terry for standing by me as I turned dreams into reality.

Acknowledgements

This manuscript would still be an undeveloped plan buried in the detritus of projects that I never quite get to if not for the following list of family, friends and teachers: Terry, Mom, Ian, Rachel and Neely who encouraged, read drafts and edited; Ian who staged the best graduation party ever; the staff at Don Mills Achievement Center who sacrificed so many lunch hours listening to readings of the essays as well as Master Handest who listened and read for continuity; Dan, Diane, Sue and Juilene for end-game editorial polishing; for the MFA staff at Carlow University, especially Ellie Wymard who held us all to a grand standard of excellence; my mentors, Marion Winik, Dinty Moore, Anne Enright and Conor O'Callaghan who did the best they could; and with special warmth to the Original Twelve, the first class of Carlow University's MFA in Creative Writing Program. Their acceptance of this speech therapist into their society of writers, their encouragement and support, suggestions and nudgings will live forever in my heart. Go raibh maith agat.

Introduction

I grew up in East Liberty, more commonly known as 'Sliberty, one of Pittsburgh's multi-racial, multi-ethnic neighborhoods. Throughout the '40s and '50s, I roamed asphalt and red-brick labyrinths linked by alleyways and terraced hillsides. Children of all colors and sizes surged through doors and off porches, offering a wealth of playmates, adversaries and opportunities for mischief. My home, 6333 Glenview Place, was a middle house in a row of four dwellings. A thin party-wall separated us from the DeFillipos on one side and the Borassos on the other. I rarely felt alone on my block.

It was a different story in school. My parents believed that I would get a better education in a parochial school. So I traveled out of the neighborhood to attend Sacred Heart School. School was a world apart, a world I tolerated only until the 3:00 bell signaled my escape back to my real life. Our parents were determined that my sister and I would find a better life through education. With their tireless encouragement, I managed to graduate from Sacred Heart Academy and followed my sister to Mount Mercy College where I found speech therapy, the love of my professional life.

After college I found and married another love, Terry Ashbaugh, a high school social studies teacher and confirmed country boy. Terry had a job teaching in a kindergarten-through-twelfth-grade school in the rural community of Tidioute, Pennsylvania. Looking forward to new adventures, I left industrial Pittsburgh and followed the Allegheny River north to settle in a small town where the same river courses through farmlands and wood stands. Here it ran clean and wild, with heron and deer feeding along its banks. After years of living in close quarters with friends and neighbors, I thrived among trees, fresh air and open spaces.

When I arrived, a speech therapy position in the local school district was open and waiting. Among the eleven schools on my new schedule was Plank Road, a one-room schoolhouse. I couldn't believe such a place still existed in 1967 America.

On the appointed day of my first visit to Plank Road, I nosed my blue Volkswagen up the steep grade of route 337, where it leaves route 62, just past the bridge that connects Tidioute with the rest of the world. If those East Liberty denizens could see me now! After what seemed an unreasonably long drive past dozens of uninhabited hunting camps, I turned into the driveway that led to a white, wood-sided building with green trim. It looked like a slightly larger hunting camp, except for the playground equipment set in a clearing, backed by the deep green of a hemlock stand.

The teacher, Peg Marshall, met me at the door with the warm cheer of a farm wife welcoming her new neighbor. Peg was a tiny lady with a calm, professional bearing. She said that she was delighted to have someone come in once a month to take over her class, freeing up some time for paperwork. I panicked, tried to calm my voice and explain that I was clinically trained, not a teacher, but a therapist. I worked with two or three kids at a time. I didn't do classes. Peg smiled and assured me that the older students would help. She said that she would send the kids out to the playground, and we could go over her lesson plans.

I stood, tucked against the blackboard for support. My mouth opened but nothing sensible came out. Peg lined up the class and went to the door. Swinging it open, she stopped, put her hands on her hips and said, "Oh, look! That mama bear is out there doing her doo-doo on my playground again." She grabbed a broom, ran out sweeping the air in front of her, and chased a lumbering black bear into the woods. One of the older boys was sent out, equipped with a huge coal shovel, to scour the playground for bear poop.

I cried all the way home that evening and told Terry we would stay two years to his tenure, then we were out of there. I couldn't live in a place where black bears pooped under jungle gyms.

Weeks grew into months. Semesters came and went. Ian was born, followed by Rachel and Neely, three kids in five years. I started working on my master's degree and the ease of rural life seeped into my soul.

We will celebrate our 40th wedding anniversary this June. We have both retired from gratifying careers, sent three children off into the world and still live in Tidioute. The enchantment that bewitched my heart and lured me into permanent residence was largely the abundance of nature that thrives within sight of my kitchen door and the wonderful freedom I have to walk out of that door and explore a world I barely knew existed as a child.

The woods bristle with the cool fragrance of early fall. Day by day I measure summer's waning as the sun slides lower along the horizon in the darkening evenings. We begin our descent down through the woods behind the pasture, following a steep deer-path cluttered with leaves and twigs scattered by yesterday's storm. Images of branches dance along the trunks of great oaks like Indonesian shadow puppets. The three dogs scout ahead, running nose-down, crisscrossing patterns, adding a certain canine intensity to our daily walk. A steady press of wind pushes through swaying trees, warning of the approaching storm.

In the old farmhouse below, three generations go about their evening routines. My mother, who lives with us, will be nervous that we're still out so close to dark. My daughter, Rachel, and her husband, Matt, are with her, having temporarily moved in as Matt furthers his education. My son, Ian, and his wife, Becky, will visit later with their newborn, Kai Kennevan. My youngest daughter, Neely, lives in southern Ohio with her husband, Eric, and their two children, Jacob, called

Jake, and Madeline Rose. When they visit for a weekend, the old pre-Civil War farmhouse throbs with noisy vitality.

I'm sometimes stunned to find myself close to the top end of these generations. Now in my sixties, I wonder where the thirties, forties and fifties have gone. The growing years of childhood, and the preparation years of college thrive vividly in memory. But the times of raising children and building careers are hazy, like images in a high-speed video that blur by, pause for brief moments of focus, then spin off.

From where I stand now, I find patterns forming through these generations, creating a living history of personalities. My daughter has my grandmother's laugh, my son, my father's attitude and bearing. Little gestures, preferences, habits percolate upward to posterity. These phenomena could pass by unnoticed, beautiful artifacts of an earlier time, overlooked by their owners. However I believe fiercely in the need to awaken and sustain family history. Our chronicle is a vital tether to the soil of our past, providing a deep sense that there is a place to always call home, the place where family is found.

Enjoying a hot air balloon ride at the state fair, riders line the railing of a gondola that ascends beyond the noise and random business of the festival. The rider views distant mountains, bright bodies of water and vast farmlands. A stout tether links the balloon to the landing target below. Yet as long as that tether connects with the earth the experience is just a carnival ride. A strong family provides the courage to sever that tether, allowing the balloon to drift off to the hills, lakes and countryside, always with the assurance that when the balloon chooses to return to its landing site, someone will toss a rope and tie it down.

For generations the lore, customs and traditions of our family have provided this security freeing the bravest of us to venture beyond the ordinary.

Rose Kennevan-Ashbaugh

Tidioute, Pennsylvania

March 2008

One Shot

I start in October. In early fall the rut stirs the herd into new patterns of activity and there are few weekends left to study them. As I stalk toward the woods, the sun still warms my back. I slip into the shelter of trees at pasture's edge. A worn path, overgrown with browning ferns, leads from the hemlock stand through a sunny clearing into dense thorn – apples. Here and there a faint crescent etches the mud, each hoof print telling a story of species, size, direction and speed. A mound of shiny black pellets lies on a mat of gold and crimson leaves. It looks fresh. I stoop and lay the back of my index finger across the pile. Cold, stiff, left this morning. They'll pass this way again.

I learned to hunt when my country boy husband and I moved to the wilderness of northwestern Pennsylvania. I learned to hunt with men. They engaged in complicated group drives and tracking parties. They felt compelled, in their chivalrous, condescending way to try to dress and drag my kill for me. It's my kill, I'll gut it myself, thank you. That's part of the process. It dilutes the accomplishment if not performed by the shooter, as if you had hooked a blue marlin and let someone else reel it in. So after picking up the basics, I chose a more solitary style.

My breath slows. I become a shadow lurking downwind of the trail. Twilight advances, lingers, crawls among the trees, erasing shadows. I watch. A solitary doe, stepping cautiously, emerges on my left. Then, a gathering of five more deer materializes, moving step by deliberate step toward a ragged, post-harvest cornfield, and their evening meal. I begin to shiver with the evening chill. Time to go home.

After six weeks of reconnaissance I choose my stand, a convergence of three trails that I can readily find in the dark. Opening day of buck season falls on the Monday after Thanksgiving. I'm in the woods before daybreak. I clear a spot, brushing snow from the leafy forest floor. Still, jacket scratching rough oak bark, rifle tucked, barrel up, against my shoulder, I catch the sweet scent of gun oil mixed with pine and leaf mold. Sweating from the exertion of walking through deep snow, I quietly unzip my blaze orange jacket and turn slightly into the wind, flirting with its chill caress. With a deliberate, frosty exhale, I watch and I wait. As I scan the darkness, a dull orange haze tints the horizon. The blush spreads, separating trees from rocks and sky. Minutes pass. I hear a sound, a soft swish, not a rustle, not a crunch, the whispered brush of hoof sinking into snow followed by the soft snap of a frozen twig. Alert, senses aroused, only my eyes shift toward the sounds.

At first, one doe drifts into view. Soon three more appear, walking, single file, along the trail. Breath controlled, my thumb firmly nudges the safety. I hold, anticipation tensing my body, breath shallow and rapid. Barely visible through the mist a fourth deer lags behind. Tension builds. How long can I hold the urge to move in check?

The fourth deer edges into range, proud under his six-point rack. Fighting a surge of excitement, slowly, deliberately, I slide the butt of the Remington 243 against my right shoulder and press my cheek into the smooth wood. Breath fast and shallow, I focus in the scope, sight lowered, slight shift left, rifle steady. Inhale. Exhale half way. Squeeze the trigger. A startling explosion rends the air. One deer drops out of sight. Others scatter, crashing through the trees. Heart pounding, I force myself to hold my stand, too quick a move could cause a wounded animal to run, second to second, breath ragged now, heaving with barely leashed excitement. Okay now, now, I roll away from the oak and step toward a brown mound framed in red splattered snow. I approach cautiously, rifle at ready. No movement, I poke the eye with my barrel, no movement. He's dead, one clean shot behind the front leg. A sense of raw power releases an orgasmic shudder through my viscera.

I drop to my knees in the snow, exhausted, spent, caressing his still warm body, running my hand along his neck down to the neat little hole in his shoulder. You're dead. You're mine. I rock back on my heels and as I peel off fleece shooting mitts a bitter shock of cold wind stings my naked skin. I slip my skinning knife from its sheath and, spreading the stiff, short fur on his chest, press the tip into the flesh at the base of his breastbone.

A chickadee sings her egocentric, five-note eulogy. Sounds of life return to the woods.

Hey, Joe!

We sit on the floor of the turtle room, our name for the speech therapy office at the Don Mills Achievement Center. Don Mills is a not-for-profit association that supports a unique, special-needs preschool, where I am employed part-time as a speech pathologist. I work with four remarkable women: Barb, our director, who labors tirelessly to keep us fiscally sound; Amy, a bright, intuitive special ed teacher; Mary Ann, who wears many hats – secretary, classroom aide, bargain shopper – and Ann, our classroom aide and diaper changer.

We arrange ourselves, four adults and seven preschoolers on the gray Berber carpet, grouped in a chaotic, sort-of-circle that changes shape each time a child's attention wanders off with his body in tow. A fiber-optic Santa, Kwanza candles and menorahs decorate the room, with Dora, SpongeBob and Bob the Builder scattered randomly on windows, doors and in the toy crate. Nemo, our pet red-eared slider, slips off his green, plastic turtle island to splash in the fluorescent-lit aquarium.

Today in Turtle Time, our euphemism for speech class, we sing our days of the week song and recite a rhyme about "eight little reindeer pulling Santa's sleigh." Each child takes a turn reaching into a gift-wrapped box to select an "R" picture and practice saying the word. R is for reindeer, Rudolph, wreath, (they can't spell yet), ribbon.

Turtle Time seems rushed and haphazard today. Everyone knows that when it's over, we will clatter down the hall to the playroom and join parents, grandparents and siblings for the annual Christmas party.

Olivia, conspicuously absent earlier, arrives late; very unusual, as her mother is conscientious about attendance. Olivia joins the rest of the kids, seeking out her special friend, Tara. Both girls are dressed in bright red-and-white Christmas skirts and sweaters. As usual, Tara has stashed her prosthetic arm in her cubby. Her knit sleeve flaps loosely as she skips hand in hand with Olivia. Olivia's thick, auburn curls sway with the rhythm of their friendship dance. Olivia's mom stands apart. She catches Amy's eye and they step into the hall.

The party winds down. Amy looks glum as she helps Santa gather his empty bag and slip out the door to his pickup. Empty trays of broken pizza crusts and cookie crumbs lie deserted on the snack table, as families, fussing with coats, boots and backpacks, say their "goodbyes" and "Merry Christmases." Olivia's mom takes my hand and leads me away from the cubbies. She says that she has something to tell me. She is agitated. Her hands move randomly. She tells a story about her adult son and Olivia. She explains how Olivia now owns a piece of the adult world that no four year-old girl should be burdened with. Olivia knows about oral sex. She doesn't know how to say it. She knows how to do it. She was taught by her older brother. She was taught in what should have been the sanctuary of her own home. Her mom wants advice. Amy has already told her what must be done, but Olivia's mom is reluctant to involve agencies. She wants another option. There is no other option.

The staff gathers in the kitchen. The families are gone. We are furious, sick, angry, frightened, frustrated. Our eyes well. Our fists clench. Olivia's mother told us that the brother had been raped himself as a child. And so it goes, generation to generation. That's not an excuse. It can never be an excuse.

We're supposed to go out for our holiday luncheon. Instead we sit in the kitchen and talk about Olivia. We talk a lot at Don Mills. That's how clusters of women work things out. Language is our unifier, our problem solver and our solace. While I share in the conversation, there is a secondary discussion going on in my mind, a quiet debate. I want to present colleagues with another shading of this picture. Could they understand it today, when the shock is so fresh? The story that I want to tell is about the day I baked a birthday cake for a rapist, how I saw the innocent smile when we sang to him. I hugged him. I put my arms around him, and comforted him even though I knew that he had violated his girlfriend's twelve-year-old daughter.

They're all too unnerved to get it right now, or am I too reluctant to bring it up? Rose Ashbaugh, consummate story-teller, backing away from an opportunity to tell a good tale? Something doesn't make sense here.

When all that can be done is done, we gather our teacher-presents and cards with crayon-scrawled names, letters inverted and scattered, give hugs and drift, one by one to the parking area.

I drive home that night in the solitude of my SUV, listening to "Drive Time Italian," my CD-based language course. Listening to the dialog, I drift back to the vocal rhythms that formed the refrains of my childhood. Then, perspective takes the shape of a minor epiphany.

I didn't tell the "good tale" at Don Mills today because the other women know nothing of my grandfather, and to understand the birthday cake incident, they have to understand my relationship with a man who immigrated from Naples over a century ago. My grandfather was not a deviant like Olivia's brother or the pedophile, but he was a harsh disciplinarian who deeply wounded his child.

When Joe Napolitano walked ashore at Ellis Island in 1901, he was 16 years old, the youngest of three brothers born on a vineyard in Cicciano, Naples. The vineyard was small, too small to divide three ways. That left Joe and the middle son, Anthony, with a future no more promising than working as common laborers for their older brother. Emigration to "The Land of Gold" became the family solution and goal. When Joe, a shy, soft-spoken country boy, arrived in New York City, he was gaunt, depleted from fourteen days of seasickness, alone and unfamiliar with the language. His first task was to find his way from New York to Pittsburgh, where Anthony had married and set up residence on Larimer Avenue in Pittsburgh's Little Italy. I never heard the story of how my grandfather made his way from

Ellis Island to East Liberty, but I know he was a proud and stubborn man, used to accomplishing whatever he set his mind to.

Joseph adopted his new country with total commitment, refused to send back to Italy for an Italian bride and would speak only English. That determination continued through my lifetime, even after his English was readily understandable and more grammatically correct than many native-born East Libertarians.

Joe bought a black Packard dump truck and contracted to Duquesne Light. He spent his off hours with his brother's family, playing cards at the Italian Club, singing and dancing. One night, at the Brynn Mar Dance Hall, he met the feisty, high-stepping Anna Sibilina Auchello. Anna was a hard-working second-generation Italian girl. She and her mother took in laundry to help support themselves and two younger brothers. Her vagabond musician father left them for long periods of time. Family lore reports that Tony Auchello had a Stradivarius that sang like angels.

Anna grew up in a neat two-story house at 6242 St. Marie St. in East Liberty, just across the Meadow Street Bridge from the Napolitano household. Joe and Anna married in 1910 and moved to 1241 Morningside Ave. where my mother, Madeline was born. For years life was good. Joe's work was steady.

Joe was destined to enjoy 73 birthday celebrations. (Birthdays were great occasions in our family; in fact birthdays *are* family.) At home in his new land, he never went back to Naples. Then in 1929, along with those of the rest of the country, his fortunes tarnished with the Great Depression. The bottom fell out of his life; Joe and Anna lost their home. By then Madeline was married to her high school sweetheart, Bill Kennevan, a six foot, blue eyed, kinky haired Irishman; not an Italian boy, but at least he was Catholic. With no other options available, Bill and Madeline welcomed her parents to move into their three-story, house on Glenview Place. Here they lived out their days as Nonie and Grandpap to my sister and me.

A quiet day. I am about eight years old, following Grandpap out of the kitchen after listening to a Pirates' baseball game on the radio. Grandpap usually sat in a rigid metal chair with his red plastic radio perched close to the edge of the kitchen table. He would lean into the radio as if he could see through the mesh-covered speaker right into Forbes Field. He wore his usual crisply pressed tan Sears and Roebuck work pants and white cotton shirt.

I measure my steps to match his. Close behind, I smell his Aqua Velva. Please don't go upstairs, I'm thinking. Go to the porch. Smoke your pipe. Please.

He strides to the front porch. The breezy, closed-in room fronts onto Glenview Place, a narrow dead end street bordered by red brick row houses on one side and newer, free-standing single residences on the other.

I slip a little white book off the shelf. Grandpap drops stiffly into the overstuffed cushioned seat of a forest green wicker chair. Flies ping off the window screens seeking cool shelter from their brick and concrete world.

I sit on the floor and pretzel my legs. The woven hemp rug is scratchy on my skin. He smiles and takes the book. I lean against his legs. His pants still smell like Nonie's hot iron.

He lights his pipe. The fruity fragrance drifts from a smoky cloud ebbing above his head. He opens the shiny white cover of the book, brought from Italy by a relative, years ago.

I hear my friends. They're playing on the street. Got their bikes racing around the cars. I don't care. I feel good here. I like it when just the two of us talk and read.

Grandpap holds the book open on his lap, one hand resting on my short mass of curly brown hair. He points to the picture of the brave little black boy who defiantly stands his ground against a hungry, toothy crocodile and reads, in Italian. The tones of an unlikely duet between Nonie and Old Blue Eyes drift from the kitchen while Mario Lanza's "O Sole Mio" leaks through the party wall that separates our home from the DeFillipos next door.

Grandpap reads in Italian. Then he recites the same words in English. I feel proud when he says Italian words to me; important, loved and secure.

My grandfather, immigrant, truck driver, family man – and, as I learned as a teenager, abusive parent. He was certainly not a rapist but his daughter carries the pain of his harshness into her ninth decade. My grandfather's hands, hands that cruelly slapped my mother, caress my hair, hide my Hershey bars behind the cookie jar. Those same hands brutally forced my mother to hold back the soft heads of baby rabbits while he slashed their throats. At ninety-two, she still shivers at the memory of the blood staining their brown fur as she felt life drain from their bodies. She was forced to gag down the meat at dinner that evening.

My grandfather's feet, feet that kicked my mother down a flight of concrete steps, rest, slippered in soft brown leather, blue-veined and vulnerable.

My grandfather's voice, the voice that shouted unforgivable words to an errant teenager, reads lyrical words of bravery, words that make me feel loved.

Does that help explain why I bake cakes for the odds and ends of humanity? I met Fred, the abusive man whose memory invaded my thoughts earlier today, in a parenting class that my husband, Terry, and I taught for court-ordered perpetrators. The day I brought in a cake for Fred's birthday, Paul, the supervising caseworker, came in at the end of class for his usual debriefing. I offered him a piece of cake. He tore into it with gusto. I told him it was for Fred's birthday. His fork seemed to wedge itself in cement frosting. Paul was an ex-collegiate wrestler, still young enough to be hugely muscular. His massive head fringed with thick, black curls swiveled sideways like a curious grizzly. He didn't seem to be able to think of anything to say.

Thinking a caseworker would understand, I explained that I could be so tolerant with words that were put in my head by the Sisters of Mercy, my teachers. I said that I looked into Fred's eyes and found the face of God, the piece of the image of the Creator that is in each of us. I said that God loves us all, my children and husband, and mother, and Jeffry Dahmer, and Adolph Hitler and rapists.

Paul didn't believe it. He took his paper party plate with its half eaten occupant and left the room. Perhaps I should have told him about my grandfather first.

This is why I can bake unearned birthday cakes, why I can see, but not justify, another side to Olivia's story, why I want to tell my tale to people who are important to me. A man can be cruel to his daughter. That same man can age into a loving grandparent, shaping the personality of an independent tomboy, giving her the time and attention that other adults were too busy to spare.

My grandfather gave me the gift of love, of learned self-worth, and planted seeds of tolerance in my heart, even tolerance that seems undeserved.

Looking for Leah

We became a foster family in 1974. Of the twenty-seven children who shared our lives over the next two decades, those most damaged were children who had lost a mother. A missing father leaves a gnawing pang, but an absent mother is an insatiable pit in the child's emotional gut. Actually, I knew this long before we began fostering. My own father searched all his life for bits and pieces of his lost mother, Leah Kennevan, to fill the void her absence left in his soul.

In the second decade of the twentieth century, Dan Kennevan and his brother Tom moved from their birthplace in Philadelphia to Pittsburgh to take advantage of the bottomless fount of highly-paid jobs in the rapidly industrializing city. Tom introduced Dan to Leah Sunderland. Leah was seven years Dan's junior and came from an affluent Protestant family who vehemently opposed their relationship. Leah stood up to them and married her wiry, jovial, Irish-Catholic love. Dan Kennevan made people smile. He was fun to be around. Unfortunately, his charms were lost on Leah's brothers, who never came to terms with the union.

Around 1909, Dan further isolated Leah from her family with the decision to move to San Francisco, where jobs were also supposed to be plentiful, as the city was still cleaning up and rebuilding from the great earthquake of 1906. Work had also begun on the Trans-Panama Exposition. However, this time a well-paying job failed to materialize for Dan.

After a five-year sojourn in California, Dan still had yet to find a secure position and the family, now including my father and his younger brother, returned to Pittsburgh.

Life was easier for Leah with her family and friends close by. Dan found steady work in the mills and the young mother settled into a happy life raising her boys. However in 1919 a flu epidemic swept through the city infecting thousands including Leah. After a long struggle, she died in the Spring.

Even though he barely remembered her, my father spoke of his mother with reverence, telling the few stories he remembered over and over, making her part of my life.

There was an indoor swing in the basement of our house, a polished oak slab with two sections of rope tied to the rafters, made for me by my grandfather. When life upstairs became too boring or annoying, I escaped to the swing in the basement. Sailing back and forth, in an almost hypnotic state, I fantasized about Leah. I daydreamed that we sat at the kitchen table eating cookies and talking. She listened to me. We laughed.

Then, one summer evening in 1963, the fantasies became real when Dad handed me an envelope containing seven letters and as many postcards, written by Leah Kennevan from San Francisco. From 1910 to 1915, she maintained a correspondence with her aunt, Polly Sunderland, in Pittsburgh. Polly had saved those letters and cards for five decades. In the spring of 1972 she contacted my father concerning a silver tea service and opal ring that she had been holding as collateral on a loan made to Dan Kennevan after Leah's death. Dan had died over twenty years earlier, in 1942. Dad paid the debt. Polly returned his mother's possessions as well as a manila envelope containing an even greater treasure, Leah's letters.

I read the letters for the first time stretched across my bed in my parents' house in Penn Hills. My mother had recently realized her dream of leaving the row house in the city for a modern, split-entry ranch in the suburbs. Distant sirens, cicada song, and other muffled sounds of suburban life strayed past my open window; sounds of a world still moving forward in time. Leah's words were my reality that night. The aloof mystery that Leah had always been fleshed out, infused with color.

Those letters opened a passage into decades past. I could reach through and touch her: a young, homesick mother, a wife with unfailing faith in her husband, a pretty woman with no money to buy new clothes. I saw that her love for my father wasn't just a little girl's fantasy. It was an intense reality, and after years of longing for his lost parent, Dad learned, from her own words, how she treasured him.

There was a picture in another envelope, old and fragile. It was labeled Leah Levina Sunderland (Birdie). Aunt Polly thought she was about fifteen in the picture. The lovely young girl had lush, brunet ringlets draped over her shoulders. She was standing at an ornate, mahogany desk wearing a dark, silk shirtwaist. A large, white lace collar split and extended down either side of her bodice. She stood in a relaxed posture, glancing down at a scroll that rested the wooden surface. Her expression was thoughtful, focused, with a touch of adolescent introspection, giving no sign of the hard life to come or her tragic end.

Leah left her family and the only city she knew to follow Dan's dream to California. She didn't seem to share her husband's love of the city, perhaps because she left more behind, a stable family and more rooted lifestyle than he had. Ever the optimist, however, Leah usually wrote home in a matter-of-fact, upbeat mood. Yet words of lonely longing and homesickness color the landscape of her brief messages. In each of her letters home, Leah hungers for contact, writes, with great affection, of mundane things from home and shares her love of her little boy, the glue that held her life together.

San Francisco Cal

March 2, 1911

Dear Lena

I just got your letter this morning and thought I would answer it right away. Well Lena the baby is doing fine he is four months old and the Dr says he certainly is an extra strong baby. Dan is just crazy over him. Dan is working to-day and all we can do is talk of home. I wish we were there now, I am going to send Mary a letter in answer to the one I got last week. Tell Poll she shouldn't go and spend her money on me, just so she gets the baby some little thing and sends Dan's ring. The baby is always laughing he is so long and such long fingers and the same shape as Elizabeth's used to be. He just went to sleep and I hope he sleeps for a couple of hours. It is a case of wash and iron every day when you have a baby. Dan said if he happened to be near home at noon he would come home to lunch. I hope he is for I hate to eat all alone. . . . Thanks for the picture of (little) Leah I suppose I won't know her when I see her. Does she ever mention my name. Do you folks ever hear from our George I haven't heard from him since last spring. Well bye-bye with lots of love from the three kids.

Before the family split over Leah's choice of my grandfather for a husband, her brother, William, had named his daughter Leah after her. Leah was devoted to her niece and her writings about Little Leah's death indicated the depth of the rift between brother and sister.

San Francisco

May 24 1911

Dear Poll

I received the sad news from you and Lilie both. Just to think I will never see dear little Leah again I can't realize it. I am all broke up over it she must have suffered terrible. You would have thought in a case of death that Will would have sent me word. But I am going to write to them any way as soon as I can send a little money for them to buy some flowers for the grave. Poll I am so glad Leah is buried next to mother. I didn't know she was going to school. I am going to ask them for a picture of Leah when I write I hope they won't refuse. It is very warm here to-day and I had quite a big wash so I am rather tired. The baby has five teeth now and another one about ready to come through. . . . Well Poll give our best to all I can't write very well to-day as I can't get little Leah off my mind oh if I only could have seen her. Did Will and Daisy mention my name while you were there. Write soon Poll. I will close for now. Hoping everybody is well.

*

San Francisco

July 3,1911

Dear Poll

. . . . I had his (the baby's) picture taken yesterday will send you one when they are finished. Our Will never answered my letter. I am going to send him a picture of the baby I don't know whether he will want it or not. Poll try and get our Georges address from Will for I would like to send George a picture. I haven't been able to send money to Will yet for some flowers for Leah's grave but I haven't forgotten. Maybe that is why Will hasn't written. But I couldn't spare the money in fact we couldn't spare it for the baby's pictures but we thought if any thing would happen to him it would be awful not to have a picture in fact they are only postals. . . . I wish we were out of debt and could get some clothes just think Dan is still wearing his gray suit for good. And I am wearing the blue skirt and light coat and that big summer hat I had at home you know the one I got when I got the brown silk dress I have the dress too. Just think I bought the baby shoes Sat. and we had to pay a dollar.

Years of rereading the letters left an aura of enchantment around the reality of Leah. After decades devoted to raising a family and career building, I retired and found time to flesh out the line-sketch of information we had about her. Hours of research culminated in a plan to follow Leah to San Francisco, to see what I could find of her life and experiences there.

There they were: the Golden Gate Bridge, the Dutch windmill, just as they'd been pictured on the tinted postcards she had sent ninety years earlier. At the public library, I went through tax records and found the location of the boarding house she lived in. Survey notes pinpointed the location. That city block is now part of the Moscone Convention Center. Using the return address on the envelope from Leah's letter, written days after my father's birth, I found the location of Lane Hospital, a facility built specifically for charity cases. It exists now as the California Pacific Medical Center.

We walked to city center. I paced off the steps to what would have been 292 Third Street, Leah's return address, and stopped. I was standing on the site of the boarding house where Leah, Dan and Dad lived. I stood as close as I could to the paved-over yard where Leah took my father out to play in the California sun.

The next day we took a bus to Muir State Park, the land of the great costal redwoods. We drifted along trails, inhaling the pungent fragrance of cedar. We walked among trees that were seedlings during the time the great cathedrals of Europe were under construction. They stand over 300 feet high, majestic lords ruling a peaceful kingdom, where their heady scent swirls through drifting fogs, that open in patches on the red-barked giants. I gazed up, into their canopy, and felt like a member of a tiny, insignificant, species. These trees were already ancient and huge ninety years ago, when Leah lived just forty-five minutes away.

The air that my grandmother breathed just several miles down shore could have drifted on currents shared by these trees. Nine decades later, I felt invigorated by the clean, cool oxygen of those same redwoods.

San Francisco

Sept. 14, 1911

Dear Poll,

I received your letter the other day and was sorry to hear of Lena not being well. Poll you are welcome to come and live with us all your life time if you want to and as to paying us board forget it as long as you can keep yourself in clothes you are welcome to whatever we have. The baby has eight teeth now and takes a few steps by himself with out holding on to anything, his hair is getting curlier every day. Dan had an accident the other day driving a wagon, the horse ran away and upset the wagon and Dan went in under the wagon and Mrs. Murrays little boy was on the wagon and he got hurt pretty bad but is doing fine now.

> *Dan got all bruised and cut but he managed go to work how he worked is more than I can tell for he could hardly walk. More darn holidays here than enough Dan says if the Mayor of the city wants to go to the toilet they hold a holiday just like Dan isn't it . . .*
>
> *As ever love to all.*
>
> *Your kids Birdie Dan & Kenneth*

Family history reports that Poll never took Leah up on the invitation to come to San Francisco.

When I was very young I pretended Leah loved the marigolds we planted on her grave. She was an imaginary guest that I read to on the couch and chatted with in the basement on my swing. When I was older and saw her picture for the first time, I was certain I could see a resemblance between her and my father.

For his seventieth birthday, I made Dad an album containing her letters, postcards and pictures. He unwrapped it sitting in his lounge chair in front of the picture window in the living room. He opened it and turned the pages slowly, carefully. When he closed the last page he set the book on his lap, both palms resting on the cover. He said nothing.

It was in his eyes, those robin's-egg-blue eyes that were his dominant feature. He stared past the TV. I think he was seeing other rooms, in orphanages, coal town shanties, foster homes, rooms he grew up in without her.

The Turtle Room

Early on a cold, snowy January morning I make the steep descent off Babylon Hill on a narrow country road that runs through forested land, broken by occasional hunting camps and unimposing residences. The chill black sky presents brilliantly-lit constellations that seem to hang within reach. In ten minutes I cross the ice-laced Allegheny and pass into hibernating farmland. Soon the sun breaks over the horizon, illuminating thousands of tiny ice diamonds sprinkled across snow-covered corn fields. I pass intervening wooded areas where naked hardwoods team with the cool, orange sun to strobe my windshield like a huge disco ball. As I crest the peak of Preston Road, just minutes from my destination, the truck cab is invaded by a cell phone singing "Ode to Joy." Caller ID shows my daughter Rachel's number.

Rachel's husband, Matt, has arrived home from his trip to Fort Stewart, Georgia. He went to help his youngest brother, Zach, prepare to leave for Iraq on his second tour of duty. As he speaks, I pull into a parking slot beside our preschool at Warren State Hospital's geriatric building. The yellow brick, one story building has trapezoidal, flat – topped roofs on each wing, now decorated with startlingly thick, gray, ice columns. Matt takes over the phone to say hi. I ask how his family is holding up and he says pretty well.

Zach, the only one of three brothers to have children, needed help resettling his wife and sons in Conneaut Lake, PA after his deployment. This would place Robin within easy reach of her family and friends. Matt, his brother, John, and their father, Mike, met in Georgia to bring Robin and her two little boys home to Pennsylvania.

Matt seems eager to describe their last hour with Zach. They drove into a surreal scene of desolate, regimented rows of tan, military style, doublewide trailers, many abandoned by earlier departures of forces. Vast, empty parking areas stretched before them, as their usual occupants-mechanized infantry, Bradleys, Abrams and Humvees-had already been shipped. Scattered across this gravel moonscape, a few flatbed railroad cars waited to load the remaining vehicles. In the center of the assembly area rose a mountain of rucksacks and framed M.O.L.L.E. packs bundled with double strands of colored packing tape, orange, white, green, red, yellow, each unit having its own identifying colors to mark their gear. Around this growing mound of baggage, families clustered in those little huddles that families gather into for wartime goodbyes. After what Matt describes as an emotional parting, Zach turned and strode toward the weapons locker, the area of demarcation separating soldiers from civilians. The minivan carrying his family pulled out of the parking area trailing other departing families off base and into the edgy days that stretched ahead.

Matt sounds weary now. We hang up. I slide out of the truck, gathering my speech therapist's trappings, computer bag, Bob the Builder backpack, purse, lunch and a handful of valentines to be laminated for today's "Turtle" drills. I dance my usual shift-and-juggle routine to unlock the door, step inside the empty building and throw the switches that flood our wing of the old geriatric center with light. I enjoy the stillness of the school in these minutes before the rest of the staff arrives. I bump along, bags swinging arrhythmically, past the toy-littered classroom, the secretary's office, where I pause to snap on the laminator, and past the special education teacher's office. Finally, I reach my room, situated at the end of a long hall decorated with number fish, alphabet animals and birthday turtles. I enter my office, the Turtle Room, and hear the sound of Nemo's pump flushing over his green plastic island, and the hum of the motor in the river tank across the room. There, Sticky Frog hunches on his faux rock while a swarm of guppies poke their heads against the aquarium glass in anticipation of their morning ration of stinky brown flakes. After consigning bags and computer to their appropriate stations, I smell the heat of the laminator down the hall, gather my valentines and carry them to Mary Ann's office.

As the laminator presses sheet after sheet of red paper hearts, I remember the year that I invented these valentine-shaped sentence builders. They were for Jason, my first autistic child. Jason was a lanky, blond-haired boy with a high-pitched voice that we never shushed in our desire to encourage him to communicate. We met when Jason began kindergarten. He was a remarkably hyperactive, uncoordinated little fellow with an ever-present, toothy smile. After months of struggling, drilling, cajoling and rewarding, Jason began using real words in real sentences. Our greatest progress came through my discovery of an enticing method for making communication tolerable for Jason. We learned to stand face to face, knees slightly bent and, bouncing up and down, rhythmically chant: " Hel-lo-what-is-your-name?" "My-name-is Ja-son-what-is-yours"? By spring of his kindergarten year, Jason had progressed to a level so advanced that I could consider refining his sentence structure.

One area of pronoun drill concerned his "me" for "I" substitution. Therapy now dwelt in an unstable zone between correction and reinforcement. Jason was using enough language for me to shape and correct errors. However, therapy that was too direct could cause a long, noisy meltdown and cost days rebuilding trust. "Me go lunch." "Me have snack?" were the major components of Jason's spontaneous repertoire.

On a day in early May that was warm enough for us to be sitting out on the playground for our session, Jason suddenly stood up and, for the first time mumbled, "Me go pee pee!" I, deliriously flushed with a sense of success and accomplishment, took a moment to reinforce by restating, "I go peepee," then grabbed his hand and headed for the restroom. We bounced up and down along the way reciprocally chanting "I go peepee!" "I go peepee." When we reached the bathroom I sent Jason in, and remained in the hall bouncing and chanting through the closed door, "I go peepee!" " I go peepee!" Mr. McCullough, the principal, walked by at that moment and helpfully suggested, "You could use the faculty lounge, Mrs. Ashbaugh."

Jason and I traveled a long way from that first year. We were together until fifth grade when his father, a Methodist minister, was transferred out of state. By then Jason was a gangly eleven-year-old. His smiles were less frequent. Having become aware of how different he was, Jason also became more wary of life's surprises. Through the years Jason included a small group of supportive peers into his sphere. They accepted, protected and guided him in areas where grownups couldn't. When Jason left, I missed our high energy, enthusiastic sessions, embarrassing as they may have been at times, and wonder where his road has taken him.

With neatly plasticized valentines in hand, I return to my office. The entry door down the hall slams shut and I hear Amy call hello as she heads for her office. Each heart has a picture of an L word attached to it: Little Mermaid, Lion King, lemon, lizard, lumpy. We study L in February because L is for "love". Later, when the kids come in for Turtle Time, they will find the hearts and practice their L words. We will recite love poems and learn how to sign "I love you" with our fingers, and we'll wish for more love in the world.

It's now 8:30 a.m. and the vans are lining up in the driveway. Before leaving my room, I quickly set out cans of turtle and fish food so today's special helper can feed Nemo and the guppies when the class comes in for Turtle Time. Nemo was born with a deformed flipper; previous owners called him Stubby. Our staff thought that insensitive, especially in a special-needs preschool. He was renamed Nemo after the little, fin-challenged clown fish in the popular child's movie.

Nemo is a seven-inch-long, red-eared slider, a very active reptile and an enticing pet to lure shy three year olds into my office for therapy and assessment sessions. In most clinics this kind of office is called the Speech Therapy Room. Special circumstances in our area made that title problematic. In our county, we have an early intervention program that enables therapists to service children in their homes, from birth until they reach preschool eligibility at three years of age. Some of our children are subjected to a very intense therapy program and develop strong aversions to speech therapy by the time we meet them. The very mention of the phrase "speech class" sends them into paroxysms of crying, flailing and casting their little bodies on the floor. Therefore we renamed my office the Turtle Room, where we come to do Turtle Drills; anything but the "S" word.

Three-year-old Alex is first off the van this morning. About the size of a two year old, he waddles, head down, dragging his Spiderman backpack on the ground behind him. He has dark brown hair, large round eyes to match and the chubby, pink cheeks of a toddler. Alex has been with us for five months. We have barely heard a word from him. Alex presents a condition labeled selective mutism. He can talk. He chooses not to. He plays quietly by himself and makes a tortured effort to melt into the floor when called on to be helper or respond orally. The only activity Alex enjoys is feeding Nemo and the guppies.

Alex follows directions well, until asked to speak. We used our best encouragement and security building techniques – nothing worked. We decided to get tough and made the rule that he had to at least nod his head to get a snack. That worked for a month, then he preferred to stubbornly stand on the circle carpet and watch while the others drink their white grape juice and munch granola bars. Alex will control that over which he has control-his voice. Today in Turtle Time he finds a valentine heart with a picture of a lumpy, yellow starfish on it. I say, "What is that, Alex?" He looks up with his signature innocent perplexity and clearly states, in a mildly incredulous tone, "I don't know."

The adults in the Turtle Room barely breathe, holding their collective composure. Never show excitement to a miracle. Miracles are as shy as Alex and could melt away at any moment. I softly say, "It's a starfish, Alex." Alex says, "It's a starfish." After class we line up for our usual pretend-swim down the hall, waving our turtle-flipper arms from the left side of the hall to the right side of the hall and into the playroom. Alex uses pretend flippers too. He continues to speak, joining a group of boys playing in the Scooby Doo playhouse. James, one of our more nurturing five year olds, crawls out, shouting to the adults, "Alex is talking. Alex is talking!"

Alex plays with the other kids. He climbs the wooden gym and goes down the slide. He rides the trikes, jabbering all the while. He wrestles with the others and runs in their races. At snack time, he says "please" and "thank you." He jabbers to Ann, our classroom aide, on his way back to the van.

As the vans pull away we sit, teachers, aides, therapists, at the art table, some of us in tears. What we worked for so diligently finally happened but we don't know why. What was different? What made today the day Alex chose to talk? And will he still be talking tomorrow?

The vans carry the children home. The rest of the staff leaves for the day. I have a little more to do to set up tomorrow's story time. Alone in the building again I sit at my desk, pull out theme folders and turn on the radio for company. NPR's Neal Conan is discussing the tragic day last week, January 27, the deadliest day of the war to date. Thirty-seven U.S. casualties, in separate incidents; thirty Marines and a Navy Corpsman, killed in a single helicopter crash near Iraq's boarder with Jordan. I think of Zach and Robin and the boys. I wonder how Evan got along in his new preschool today, and why his dad has to be so far away and in so much danger?

I remember the speeches I heard and the periodicals I read in the months and weeks before we invaded Iraq, before Zach left the first time. Dick Cheney said, "Simply stated, there is no doubt that Saddam Hussein now has weapons of mass destruction." Colin Powell, so trustworthy, said, "We know that Saddam Hussein is determined to keep his weapons of mass destruction and is determined to make more."

Later, after the invasion, we heard Lt. General James Conway, USMC, tell us, "We've been to virtually every ammunition supply point between the Kuwaiti border and Baghdad, but they're simply not there . . . We were simply wrong."

What sense can be made of that? Is it just another kind of Turtle Room? Is it the politician's way of re-labeling something that they can't call by its real name because everyone would just throw themselves on the floor in tears, flailing and crying? Do they avoid telling us the truth because they know that this isn't why we have baby girls and boys? This isn't why we send them to preschool to learn about love and getting along and sharing. This isn't why we raise them, not to become soldiers trained to kill and torture. This just isn't in the lesson plan.

My folders feel unimportant now. I'm tired, unfocused. I turn off the radio, pack up my computer bag, Bob the Builder backpack, purse, and empty lunch sack. With a glance back at the guppies, Sticky Frog and Nemo, I turn and head down the silent hallway, bags swaying, hungry for home.

Glenview Place

Chico, our family Chihuahua, sleeps warm against my stomach. My right hand rests on the curl of his hind leg. The left props my head. We're stretched crosswise at the foot of my parents' bed. I study my sister's reflection in the mirror of mom's big oak vanity. She sits on a wood-backed chair. The crinoline skirts of her white organza prom gown cover the front of the chair and bunch against the vanity drawer. Netting flows to the hem, decorated with dime-sized black velvet dots. Bottles of gold, blue and crystal liquids are scattered about on a glass half-shelf. Mom drapes a striped terrycloth towel over Gigi's bare shoulders. Some of the little black dots peek out around the bodice. Mom opens a drawer. Lipstick tubes rattle as a soft powdery scent drifts up. She slips out a silk blotter-cloth decorated with a mosaic of her own lip-prints and selects a gold tube of Revlon lipstick. Mom works as a Revlon representative at Sears. She gets all the newest shades. Next they brush through Gigi's curly, brown, boy-cut hair. It doesn't look any different to me, but when they finish, their faces side by side, they admire their accomplishment in the mirror.

Outside the open window, the rain eases to a gentle spatter. A wet grassy scent carries a drift of Mrs. Borrasso's garlicky onions and mushrooms frying in her kitchen next door. I'm impatient waiting for my sister to dress; Al Blank will be here soon to pick her up. Al stands tall and lean with bright red hair. I plan on marrying him some day. When he comes to see Gigi, he talks to me first. I stand tippy-toe on his shoes and we dance to Nonie's radio.

Mom is painting bright red polish on Gigi's nails. It matches her lips. They're so busy with each other, they don't seem to remember that I'm here. They talk a lot, but not to me. A feeling trickles through my belly. It's weird. My heart beats hard. I'm scared. Their voices sound like they're in another room now. "Who am I? Who am I?" The question won't stop. It spins in my head like a milkshake in the mixer at the soda fountain. I feel trapped in here. I slide off the bed. Touching the wall, I walk fast down the hall to the steps, run downstairs and head for the door. The dinner dishes are done and Nonie is laughing at something on TV as I run past.

"Where are you going?"

"Out."

She shouts something after me, but I'm across the screened porch and out the door to the front stoop before she can stop me. I hear some kids down the street. I don't want to see them. I jump down three cement steps from our front door, run past DeFillippos' stoop and down a long flight of concrete steps that connect our terrace with the sidewalk below. I run hard to the top of the street, the turn-around, where cars turn to head back down this dead-end block. The neighborhood kids have a climbing tree there. It leans over the wooded hillside that slopes down to Stanton Avenue. I touch the tree. My chest burns. I gulp air. It hurts. I climb to the big branches and sit, back against the scratchy trunk. The scared part is gone. My chest is heavy. I'm tired, and comfortable too.

I watch the roof of Al's car as he backs into the driveway under my perch in the tree. He doesn't know I'm up here. Al turns and creeps back down the street, looking for a parking space close to 6333. I twist off my branch and drop to the ground. As I cross the street Denny, standing on his front stoop, shouts, "Hey Rosie!" I smile, wave and walk on toward his terrace.

My Pittsburgh, the Pittsburgh of the late 1940s and 1950s, was a good town to grow up in. It was a hardhat, blue collar, beer-drinking town. My neighborhood was the part of East Liberty that runs from the Meadow Street Bridge to Highland Park. I lived on Glenview Place, a block long, dead end street off Heberton Avenue. My side was terraced, and featured section after section of red-brick, two-story row houses, each set of four divided from the next by a four foot wide alleyway. The alleys led to postage-stamp sized, hedge-bordered back yards. In the front, there was little more than concrete, a ragged hillside and a set of twenty-four cement steps that led down to the sidewalk and car-lined street. The single-family dwellings across the street were decades newer and had lawns and driveways. We were mostly Italian on my side, mostly Jewish across the street. There was always someone to play with. Summer nights, our imaginations came on with the streetlights. Our shabby, immigrant neighborhood grew into a jungle with lurking man eaters in the alleyways; a space academy with Captain Video and his Video Rangers, or the wild west with Annie Oakley, Wild Bill Hickok and Hopalong Cassidy. Our Schwinns were mighty steeds with flowing manes. We didn't have to wear helmets and reflectors in those days. We were free to dart in and out of the shadows in reckless pursuit. The weak were culled quickly then. Two streetlights were located one at either end of the block, leaving a delicious dark zone in the middle. The night sky pulsed orange from the stacks at J & L Steel. Only blocks away from the Highland Park Zoo, nocturnal roars and screeches rolled over the Jackson Ave embankment into our unlit back yards.

Some very special nights, Mr. Reinhardt, dressed in baggy pants, suspenders hanging from his waist, t-shirt on top, would stand in front of the second floor window and play his violin. He was a concert musician in the Old Country. We played hide-n-seek in the night to a background of Mozart, Schumann, Brahms.

Nonie and Grandpap Napolitano, my maternal grandparents, had moved in with my family before I was born. Nonie, a hot-blooded extrovert, sang, danced, played practical jokes, spoke her mind and would be, by the time I reached my teens, the bane of my social life, the terror of my boyfriends.

Nonie always made it her business to wait up for us to come home from dates. She was waiting for Gigi the night of the prom and the next morning was asking her who went with whom, who wore what. Through the kitchen window, I watched my sister carry a glass of milk out of the room. I was on the back porch, playing with my yoyo, a red and blue Duncan. Nonie won't let me play in the house. She's not fair. I practice around-the-world and walk-the-dog, waiting. Through the screen I hear Rosie Rosewell call the final play in the game at Forbes Field. A metal chair scrapes against the faded linoleum floor as my grandfather pushes away from the rectangular, plastic-covered kitchen table. KDKA's broadcast of Pirate baseball fades into Dean Martin crooning *That's Amore.* Nonie's gusty voice rises in enthusiastic accompaniment. Her gaudy, floral-print, tent-sized smock ripples like a belly dancer's beaded skirt as she stirs a pot of pasta sauce in time with her song. Her arm-waddle waves through the garlicky steam.

I slip in the screen door, slow and quiet, not letting it slam and open the refrigerator. Nonie, absorbed in her culinary dance, isn't looking. I grab a quick, cold gulp of milk, right from the bottle, two gulps, three. Then, setting the bottle quietly on the shelf, I hold the door all the way until it shuts with a soft snap. Back at the table, Grandpap reads the *Pittsburgh Press.* I sit in the chair across from him. He keeps reading. Nonie is chopping potatoes and singing *Botch-A-Me* like Rosemary Clooney, only she changes the words. I know she's singing dirty Italian words. Grandpap says, "Annie, basta!" *Basta* means enough. She sings louder. Grandpap folds the paper, pushes his chair back and leaves the room. I take a cookie from the jar. Nonie stops singing,

"Did you ask for that?"

"Can I have it?"

"It's late to ask now."

Still feeling a troubling residue from the emotions that sent me running from the house the previous night, I ask her, "Nonie, do you ever think about who you are?"

"I know who I am for a fact. Don't leave those crumbs for me to clean."

The cellar of the house on Glenview Place was remodeled into a playroom. Dad did it all himself after a job placement psychologist told him he had no aptitude for working with his hands. We had ping-pong and bumper pool tables in the main section. Tucked beside the outside stairway was a small musty bathroom with spider webs and a dull, naked bulb hanging from the ceiling. In the part toward the back of the house, past the bathroom, Nonie had her wringer washer, two laundry tubs and an old ceramic topped cook stove.

Every year, on the weekend before Easter, Nonie started making the *cavatelli*, a heavy, shell-shaped pasta served with a meaty tomato sauce. Grandpap would sit in his rocker making crosses out of the palm we gathered at Sunday mass as Nonie set out the old heavy wooden pasta board that belonged to her mother. Singing her favorite Hit Parade number of the week, adding her own words and melody, she dumped flour from a twenty-pound cloth sack, a snowy mountain, in the middle of the board. She made a dusty well in the center and added a pinch of salt and some baking powder. Then came the fun part. She cracked eggs one at a time into the well and, with a long handled, wooden spoon, stirred them into flour that drifted down the sides of the shifting mountain. The angel white powder turned a sticky, creamy yellow and bulged closer to the shrinking rim as she added egg after egg. When she set the spoon aside I knew it was my turn to start the arduous process of kneading the mass into a smooth ball. I had to stand on my chair to get enough power to punch the adhesive heap down, grab a fistful and roll it over on itself.

When my muscles gave out, Nonie took over. She pounded, slapped and rolled the mass until it submitted, transforming into a mound with a surface as smooth as a baby's cheek and the dull sheen of a frosted, glass, Christmas tree ornament. Nonie tugged off two clumps of dough, one for each of us, and threw a damp dishtowel over the rest. We rolled them into snakes, then cut off one inch lumps. We used cheese graters to shape the lumps into bumpy shells. I had a small grater, shaped like half a metal tube with a little handle at one end. With my index finger I pressed a nugget along the perforated side of the grater. The dough coiled around my finger like a soft little snail, then I shot it out the end to a pile growing in the middle of the table.

Nonie snapped out and lowered a thick cotton cloth over half of the dining room table, and sprinkled flour over it. I rubbed the flour over the cloth with my hands. Soft drifts filled in the pours in the cotton canvas, smoothing the scratchy surface. The pasta was set out on the cloth to dry. After two days they would shrink and feel as hard as chips of plaster.

On Easter Sunday morning, while even the Bunny must have been sleeping, Nonie came down to the kitchen, half ready for church. She set a huge kettle of water to boil on the stove. In slip and bathrobe, with a net over her hair, Nonie gently dropped the nuggets from a slotted spoon into the boiling water. When the pasta bobbed to the surface she stirred the steaming cauldron.

As the rest of the family trickled down, the kitchen windows steamed opaque, and tomato sauce bubbled on the back burner. The pungent fragrance of minced garlic and chopped onions mingled with mellow tomatoes and the sharp tang of oregano and basil. By the time Nonie was dressed, powdered and coiffed, the pasta was ready to be drained, mixed with the sauce, sprinkled with grated parmesan and layered into a casserole, to bake slowly while the family went off to Mass.

It Ain't My Poop

In 1999 a huge remodeling project threw the largest of my assigned elementary schools into a semester-long state of upheaval.

The art teacher became an itinerant, conducting carts filled with supplies and projects through the halls. The music teacher found herself homeless, a vagabond, roaming from room to room with sacks of instruments. There were normally two rooms per grade level; now both classes were housed in one room divided by a temporary partition. And the speech therapist (that would be me), was consigned to a kidney-shaped table in the back corner of what we call in the business, a "primary life skills room;" a room that housed the most learning disabled children in the school, children who were still working their way through basic social skills as well as gaining control of their bodily functions.

I was extremely concerned about these conditions, to put it mildly. How was I to function as a therapist with the noise and constant movement? How would my students feel about having to come to a special education room? What would their parents say? I prepared to survive the longest semester of my career.

One of the most challenging students in Sharon Persing's primary life skills class that year was Joel, a black haired, round faced, stocky boy of eight, functioning at the four to five year old level. In that year of upheaval, Joel demonstrated his objection to having his routine disrupted by soiling himself on an almost daily, basis. Sharon and one of her aides, Debbie or Carol, would change Joel. At the end of each day, he was sent home wearing a clean pair of briefs under his jeans, carrying the soiled pair in a knotted, plastic grocery bag. The new underwear was never returned. In time our backup supply ran out. Sharon sent a note home explaining the situation and asking Joel's mom to send a few sets of clean underwear to see us through the current crisis. Mom's solution was to send him to school wearing no underwear.

One morning, I sat at my speech table preparing for my next case while logging the previous session. Debbie had two students seated at their desks, completing worksheets based on a previous reading lesson. Carol had one student at a desk in the far corner, working on a math lesson. By the blackboard, in front of the room, at a long wooden table, Sharon gathered the remaining five students for a different math activity. Andrea, age eight, stopped by the therapy mirror on my table to primp.

I said, "Hi Andrea. What's up?"

Sharon called, "You're beautiful, Andrea. Your hair is so pretty. Leave Mrs. A. alone and come over here. We're learning about money."

Andrea loved money. We gave each other a high-five and Andrea joined Chuck, Steve and Noah who were seeking out the yellow and orange colored plastic chairs with their names carefully printed on the back. They chatted as they pulled the chairs to the table, jockeying for their favorite spots. Cardboard pennies, nickels, dimes and quarters were gathered in piles on the table. Joel remained standing a few feet away. Sharon began a lesson on coins with the manipulatives and worksheets. She encouraged Joel to join his friends at the table. He remained standing on his spot.

Sharon said, "Joel, your friends are waiting for you. Can you come by yourself or do you want me to help you?"

Joel stood still.

Sharon said, "Joel, we have to finish math before Miss Montgomery comes in for music."

Joel loved music.

Jason, seated at the table, leaned in to Sharon and confided, "He pooped again, Miz Persing. It's on the floor. I seen it happen."

Sharon looked up. Joel was now rocking from side to side with a pile of poop between his feet like a penguin sheltering his chick.

Joel quietly stated, "It ain't my poop."

Jason replied in a louder voice, "Yep, it is Joel. I seen it roll down your pants and hit the floor. It's your poop, Joel. It's his poop, Miz Persing."

Sharon set pennies and nickels in combinations and instructed the seated students to count them as she stood to go to Joel. Debbie, whose students were actively engaged in their reading worksheets, motioned that she would take care of it. Sharon sat back down.

At that point, Andrea, our joyfully inquisitive Down Syndrome girl, left her seat, turned to Joel and, squatting over the brown pile between his feet, sniffed. She gagged, stood and, in a strangled voice, croaked, "Yep, it's poop, yack!" and ran for the trash can. Carol rushed over to help Andrea and Debbie came forward to assist with Joel.

Chuck, running long, graceful fingers through his rumpled blond hair, squeaked his chair back and stood. Sensing an uncomfortable situation, Chuck went for his usual escape route. He asked to go to the bathroom. Absently, Sharon handed Chuck the wooden restroom pass while correcting Jason's pile of coins.

Debbie offered Joel a paper towel to clean up the poop. Joel continued rocking back and forth, chanting in a deep, monastic monotone,

"It ain't my poop. It ain't my poop."

Chuck rushed in from the restroom flapping his arms and whined, "I can't go in Miz Persing. It growled at me. The toilet's growling."

Growling restrooms were not uncommon in Chuck's autistic world. I stood, walked past Joel and the offending, orphaned poop, took Chuck's hand and escorted him to the rest room. If I stood outside the door, it stopped growling.

While waiting for Chuck, I watched Debbie come out of the classroom across the hall, with her hand on Joel's shoulder. Joel carried a clean pair of jeans and the

Batman briefs that Sharon bought at K-mart, out of her own pocket of course. The generous $50 budget allotted for classroom supplies had been consumed shortly after Labor Day.

Chuck and I returned to the room. A latex-gloved Sharon knelt on the floor, cleaning up the abandoned pile of poop with paper towels and sanitary spray. She stated, looking over her shoulder toward the three students at the table,

"Now put two dimes and a nickel by the quarters."

As Chuck sat down, Jason, ever involved in other students' affairs, pitched in to help him catch up by ordering his coins for him. Carol walked over to the table with a still pale Andrea. Settling her back into a chair, Carol couldn't help noticing the murderous look Chuck was aiming at Jason. Carol defused the situation saying,

"Thank you for helping, Jason, but Chuck needs to learn how to do it himself."

With a satisfied grin Chuck scattered the organized cardboard coins and began to rearrange them himself. Jason shot him a lip pursed look of disgust.

Debbie escorted a freshened and smiling Joel into the room. With no word spoken, he knelt down beside Sharon, ripped a paper towel from the roll and helped her dry the floor. Joel and Sharon returned to the table together. Steve and Noah made room for Joel and his chair and shared their coins with him, while Sharon began at the beginning with five pennies and a nickel.

Debbie returned to her two students. Carol resumed her explanation about taking away and adding back kittens in a basket.

As the classroom activity settled into a quiet routine my fourth grade client walked in to cheery greetings from the class. She smiled, said, "Hi guys," and stopped at Andrea's place to admire her cardboard pennies, nickels, dimes and quarters.

At most, thirteen minutes had elapsed since the beginning of the unclaimed-poop incident. Sharon still had seven minutes to finish her lesson before music class, plenty of time to achieve her planned math objectives.

As the days unfolded, the 1999 school year turned into one of the happiest and most rewarding of my 32 years as a public school speech therapist. It has long been known that life skills teachers rarely miss work. I always thought that they just didn't trust anyone else to maintain the tentative balance they work so hard to establish in their classes. From my new, more enlightened perspective I believe that it is because all of the smile and laugh-induced endorphins just make them healthier than the rest of us. That satisfaction with problems solved, goals accomplished and bright gleams of progress realized, keeps them coming back day after day. I know I never missed a day of my term in the back corner of Sharon Persing's classroom.

In that primary life skills room I learned how to juggle time, referee interpersonal conflicts in a population that feels every slight to the core and to fit square little pegs into the round holes of administrative and governmental directives.

Hovering over the keenly balanced teeter-totter of teaching, meeting standards and maintaining a happy, encouraging classroom, is the need to counsel without seeming to, to shape with great subtlety, and to accept, without rancor, negative parental attitudes.

I was gratified to watch adults (including the speech therapist) and children alike learn about kindness, patience, forgiveness, acceptance, pitching in, gentle understanding, positive discipline and the value of taking the time to find something to encourage in the people around you.

How refreshing it would be if the walls of Sharon Persing's classroom could melt away and expose the world to her curriculum. In a world where people doggedly deny what is obviously their own poop, Sharon could teach them to admit, "It's my poop alright, but I'm gonna clean it up and try not to do it again."

When the principal stopped by Sharon's room, she saw that this skilled teacher was following her daily plan appropriately and that the primary life skills class of Youngsville elementary school was learning about basic coin values. Only those of us privileged to reside in that classroom daily know what was really taught that day.

Nemo the Turtle

Nemo the Turtle,12, of 125 Hospital Drive, Warren, PA died on or about Easter Sunday, April 16, 2006, at his residence in the Turtle Room. Cause of death, undetermined. He was born in a commercial hatchery, parents unknown. He served as household pet for the White family of Warren, PA, where he was home schooled in the art of entertaining children. He graduated at age 6 and has been employed as "Classroom Turtle" at the Don Mills Achievement Center for the past six years.

He is survived by five adult keepers, and twenty preschool friends.

In lieu of flowers, memorial contributions may be made to the Home Finders Turtle Rescue fund. On the morning and afternoon of Tuesday April 18, funeral services were conducted beside the bus ramp, where Nemo was laid to rest beneath the purple pansy bed. Sort of.

I learned of Nemo's death on Easter Monday. I stopped by my office that afternoon to set up for our return to classes Tuesday morning. Amy, our special ed teacher, was already in the building. As I walked in, Tim, Amy's husband, came down the darkened hall in my direction. He wasn't moving with his usual amiable gait, his face, uncharacteristically somber. Knowing Tim, that could only mean something was wrong with Amy, the kids, or the Steelers. I could hear Amy and their two boys in her office, sounding healthy and well. Being a Steelers fan I approached cautiously. What? Roethlisberger signed with the Bills? Bettis came out of retirement to play with Cleveland?

"Hey Tim."

Tim stopped close in front of me, leaned in as if to share a secret.

"Nemo died".

"What?"

"Nemo, he's dead."

"How?"

"I don't know."

"When?"

"It's been a while."

"The boys don't know?"

"No." Tim confides, "I put him out in the field. In a month we can bring the shell back in."

"What about the mowers?"

Long pause, "They won't mow that soon." Long pause "Will they?"

"Probably."

A part of Nemo could return to the Turtle Room, like ashes in an urn. That would be nice, maybe.

In just hours school would resume. Amy and I had "a lot of splainin' to do" before next turtle time. We shelved our music and rhythm plans for an impromptu unit on death and dying.

Our first step was to secure the body. With a makeshift hazmat suit of super-sized, Ziploc baggies, Amy and I explored the grassy field in search of the spot where Tim had left Nemo's remains. With the deceased safely bagged, we returned to the agency and scrounged for a casket. Amy found an appropriate Hallmark card box with birds and flowers; classy fare for a parentless reptile. I cleaned the turtle up a bit and wrapped him in a shroud of white terrycloth dishrags.

After art time on Tuesday, I slipped out and dug a shallow grave by the playroom window.

We ended playtime early. Amy called the class over for group. They knew something was amiss. We rarely change their routine. Amy sat on her reading chair with the children scattered over the circle rug. I sat on the floor beside her, holding our books.

"Ok now, let's be good listeners." Amy used her firm but friendly teacher voice. "Rose and I want to tell you something important." Smiling, eager faces tilted up to meet Amy's eyes.

"Nemo died while we were on vacation. He isn't in the Turtle Room anymore. How many of you have had somebody you know, like a grandparent or pet, die?"

A couple of hands went up. A chatter of, "My kitty died." "Harley ran on the road." "My goldfish . . .", "Yeah my fish . . ." Others sat staring at Amy with drawn, serious faces.

Amy has a beautiful book that explains "transitions" in three-year-old terms. I read "What Does Dead Mean?" from *When Dinosaurs Die* by Laurie Krasny Brown.

We talked about new vocabulary words; grave, casket, burial, sympathy card. (Frankie, the night cleaning lady, had noticed Nemo's absence and wrote a lovely note that we read to the children). We lined up at the door and went outside. A remarkably quiet cluster of four adults and eleven children formed around the small hole. A pile of rocks stood mounded at one end. I opened the Hallmark casket. Nemo still looked fairly presentable, so I carried him by each child for a final viewing. Little fingers had to be restrained from curiously reaching out to touch.

I closed the lid and placed Nemo in his grave. Each child picked up a stone and dropped it on the casket. Michael whipped his in with a pounding thunk. Ian and Kyle followed suit before Amy snagged the next wrist and cautioned, "Gently. We bury our friend gently." We held hands and sang "Days of the Week," then went inside and down the hall to the Turtle Room, where eleven children stormed Nemo's tank.

"Not here," confirmed Michael.

"Where's Nemo?" asked Christina.

"Nemo died," I stated matter-of-factly. "We just buried him outside."

Thus began an abbreviated speech class, which ended with snack time and dismissal.

On the way to the vans, several children paused for a moment to look at the grave. Others rushed to tell drivers and parents the news. Since many of our children have speech problems, Amy had to quickly assure concerned drivers that the deceased was a pet, not a person.

Finally, the vans pulled away carrying our young mourners home or to day care.

That was the morning class. We still had the afternoon group to go. As soon as the vans were out of sight, I exhumed Nemo, cleaned his box, smoothing out the dents, and searched for a cool, shady place to store him until the next group arrived. Unfortunately, the only place out of the sun was under a window of the nursing school across the courtyard. The student nurses had been watching the morning's proceedings with mild curiosity. I learned later that they thought we were planting seeds. I smiled and waved while securing the innocuous Hallmark casket under their break-room window. They smiled and waved back, unaware of the ghoulish goings-on at the preschool across the way.

The afternoon followed a pattern similar to that of the morning. There were a few tears this time, and more questions. "Why did he die?" "But what happened to Nemo?" Someone asked if we could get a new turtle. Taylor said, "No. There's just Nemo." Amy and I agree. We need to grieve Nemo for a while. We still have the guppies, and a new colony of ants, building wonderful tunnels in their space-age, blue gel habitat.

I exhumed Nemo one final time that day. We did hope to reclaim his carapace in a month. I put him in a black, plastic microwave pan from somebody's veggie lasagna lunch, and secured him where he would remain undisturbed, in the inner courtyard. I filled in the hole, and surrounded it with stones, to hold the mowers at bay. Our director, Barb, bought some purple pansies. We planted them on the grave.

Every morning and afternoon, a few children stop at Nemo's grave to silently pay their respects, then move on with the rest of their day.

The Voodoo Passage

Kralendijk, Nikiboko, Caracara, Bananaquit. Exotic places and exotic creatures comprise the unique ecosystem of Bonaire, a semi-desert island that rests in the lower horn of a crescent-shaped archipelago known as the Lesser Antilles. Bonaire remains a possession of The Netherlands. It sits fifty miles off the north coast of Venezuela, where vast flocks of flamingos make day trips to their feeding grounds. It is an unexpected setting for my non epic odyssey through fear and into self actualization

Bonaire has lots of flamingos, more flamingos than a Florida trailer park. With the orange-pink flashes from migrating formations of these extraordinary birds and the acres of pale garnet salt flats, Bonaire blushes pink as unexpectedly as a teenage boy on his first date. Bonaire also has cactus, iguanas and pristine coral reefs. The reefs are the mainstay of tourism to the island. Say "Bonaire" to a diver and you'll see the same expression you see on the face of a chocolate lover when you say the word "Dove." The island is also home to a variety of birds, including a little green parrot with a bright yellow face called the Lori, and large, noisy parakeets.

The birds were the primary interest of our group; in fact, I was the only non-birder in a company of four that had stumbled into this island experience as a result of a gift. My son-in-law's father, Mike, and his girlfriend, Pat, are divers, who make a yearly pilgrimage to Bonaire (I use the word pilgrimage in the most classic sense. Divers are a cult.) They gave the island trip to the kids as a wedding present and encouraged us to come as well. We discovered later that our job was to entertain the newlyweds, my daughter Rachel and her husband Matt, during diving hours, which were extensive. Over the next seven days we caught only glimpses of Mike and Pat, boarding the morning dive boats and returning in late afternoon. Their evenings were spent exclusively with diving friends. Apparently, on Bonaire, there is a caste system: divers on top, followed by merchants who sell diving paraphernalia, then iguanas, wild donkeys and finally the pariahs, non-diving humans.

From our first hour on Bonaire, a bizarre tumble of color, fragrance, sound, frustration and hurt became the backdrop to my vacation from hell. Maybe it was disappointment, maybe exhaustion – we had just managed to pull off two at-home weddings nine months apart. Maybe it was voodoo, something in the spirit of the island that merged with something in my existential self

Our home for the week was the Carib Inn, a stucco, two-story building, pale cream with bright white trim. The overhanging balconies released cascading waves of fuchsia bougainvillea to the ground. Dense clusters of palm and flowering shrubs obscured the Inn and sheltered it from the road. A maze of low, stone walls defined walkways through the shrubs and trees, home to yellow, red, green and blue birds, decorating the dark, green foliage like fleeting, bejeweled brooches.

I don't dive. I struggle with an inherited fear of deep water. Watching birds gives me a headache and tries my patience. However, I do enjoy photography. From the concrete slave huts along the Atlantic shore to the irrigated gardens of the leeward shore, Bonaire presents a wealth of subjects for a photographer. With camera charged, extra battery, and memory stick, I happily anticipated each day's journey forth from our airy apartment

One of our first adventures was a trek deep into a rugged canyon, in search of nesting barn owls. The canyon was a vicious wound in the topography of the desert that forms the interior of the island. The climb down through scattered, upended boulders was brutal, more due to cactus than the rock formations. We quickly learned that there was little purchase for a safe grab to prevent downward slides or falls. A haze of silvery grey stretched from wall to wall of the canyon. Few green leaves and little bloom brightened the scene at this time of year. A wiry maze of cactus and formidable clutches of aloe clogged the canyon floor. Impenetrable stands of Divi-divi trees hunched sideways with their bare branches stretched in palsied reach, entwined in painful-looking arcs. Dull, silver masses of epiphytes hung from twisted branches, giving the impression of an old burial ground of Spanish Moss, where the trees had mummified and ghosts shrieked through the ruins.

The shrieks were actually the eerie call of a large grey-brown vulture called the Caracara. They swooped through and perched where tall, zombie – sized cacti loomed. Along the rocky ground, prickly pear cactus threw their spines into anything that even barely brushed by.

To invade this hoary, prickly territory, we had covered ourselves with long sleeved shirts and pants but the early morning temperature was already climbing into the high eighties. A breezeless, pounding, dry heat and unrelenting sun wrung perspiration from our pores. Sweat ran into our eyes. Needle-pricked sleeves and pants stuck to sweat soaked skin as we searched for the owls in their rugged habitat, catching glimpses of goats along the higher cliffs. The piercing screams of curious parrots echoed through the canyon. We trudged on, tediously scanning every hopeful site for nesting owls. No owls appeared.

Then one of the birders spotted a bright flash moving along the trees. We chased it down in a lumbering, lurching, "Ouch, damn it" sort of way. Referring to their Peterson Field Guide, Terry and the kids identified the bird as a Summer Tanager. There are no Summer Tanagers on Bonaire. Well, maybe there aren't supposed to be any. We documented the find with lots of pictures and left the desert to find some local birders who had befriended us. They were equally as startled by the tanager as by our journey into the canyon. These savvy natives said that no one ever actually goes in there-no one but goats, parrots, lizards and obsessive Pennsylvania birders. The locals scout from the perimeter, with binoculars.

Our fifteen minutes of fame grew brighter as a birding tour guide posted the find on his website. Terry, Rachel and Matt were formally credited with the historical, first sighting of a Summer Tanager on the island of Bonaire.

With the satisfaction of their accomplishment secure, the birders sacrificed the next day for me. I collect lighthouses. That is, wherever I travel, if there is a lighthouse nearby, I explore it, climb it and photograph it. Bonaire boasts five lighthouses; another reason for the excellent diving in this area of the Caribbean is the large number of shipwrecks.

Nonetheless, throughout the history of the island, the need for warning lights was critical for the safety of sailors, their passengers and cargos. We packed into our rental and left the touristy, leeward side of the island, traveling north to Washington Slagbaai Park, then along the Atlantic side, past mangroves and to the salt-pans of the south. We passed through isolated native villages and glimpsed primitive voodoo structures built along the coast, sentinels against the rages of stormy seas. I captured the formal lighthouse in the town of Kralendijk, and moved on to the slender white and red towers that rise in stark relief against the sea.

Approaching Lima, we experienced a pleasant change from the previous day's monochrome desert. Solar salt flats stretched out in shades of ever darkening pinks. The reddish coloration of the salt is caused by the presence of astronomical numbers of microscopic, salt-loving critters, called halobacteria. These bacteria produce a red carotenoid pigment. Small shellfish that live at the bottom of the ponds eat the bacteria and, in time leave their pink residue in the salt.

These same creatures are responsible for the classic color of flamingos. I was surprised to see that juvenile flamingoes are the same grey color as the desert trees. After three years of eating the halobacteria-infested shellfish, mature birds take on their characteristic coloring.

After the pleasant lighthouse tour, we returned to the apartment in late afternoon and decided to snorkel off the Carib Inn beach. My love-hate relationship with water is family legend. Like pi or infinity, most people know it exists but few understand it. With a wet suit for security, and time to acclimate, I enjoy snorkeling. My rules are simple. I have to gradually swim out from shore, and I need to be within reach of something buoyant, like my husband's butt.

Our beach opened immediately onto a striking expanse of coral. As the water deepens, parrot fish, blue tangs, queen angle fish, dart, hover and flash through swaying, orange cup coral and anemones. Bright gobys, the neighborhood clowns, swam up and peeked into our masks. I grew comfortable in an alien element.

The next morning, while shopping at the local fruit market, I saw a poster advertising a Zodiac turtle watch off Kline Bonaire, a small isle off the leeward side of Bonaire. I love sea turtles. They don't live in deserts and you can see them without binoculars. Everyone met the suggestion of a turtle tour the next day with happy enthusiasm. We signed up, paid our fee and met the skipper early Wednesday morning.

We shared our tour with a friendly threesome from Peru. I clutched my flippers, mask and snorkel and slid into a snug nook on the rubber floor of the boat. When our skipper stopped the Zodiac 75 feet off shore, the others slipped on their fins, set their masks and rolled into the sea. I slipped on my fins, set my mask and froze into a pillar of fear. I shook my head, clung to the slippery rubber edge and gulped,

"I can't do this. I have to start from shore."

The skipper calmly said, "Ok, I'll run us in. You get out where I anchor the boat."

Simple, easy, accommodating; with relief, I watched the bobbing heads of my family and three Peruvians shrink away, as we motored to the edge of Kline Bonaire. The skipper slid out of the boat and set out to secure an anchor.

He said, "The coral's sharp. Just start swimming back. I'll catch up."

I started off, satisfied to be heading out toward the others, happily scanning the ocean floor for turtles. My erstwhile skipper never reappeared. I focused down and swam on. I would find them on my own. I would not give up. I had already wimped out once. I wouldn't do it again. When the tide pushed me too close to shore, submerged fields of bottles, cans and discarded tires cluttered my view. Stinging, bright orange fire coral bloomed along the edge of the dumps. I turned out to deeper water, the clean ocean floor falling further from sight. I could hear my breath hissing through the snorkel, growing shallow and rapid. I measured the thrust of my fins and sweep of my arms, deliberately slowing my breath, listening as the hollow hiss evened out in the gurgling black tube. The sound of my own breathing and the bubbly churn of my limbs moving through the water were solace and company. I moved steadily on. An isolated, lonely feeling surrounded me. Then I heard a strange growl, deep, throaty.

"Oh shit, what's that?"

I was alone. I listened. The growl blended with my exhales, and silenced with each inhale.

"Oh man, it's me. No crying. Damn it, Rose, no crying. Smooth breathing. Go cold. Go calm."

The groans stopped.

"This is too long. God, where am I?"

The waves grew large, strong. They were breaking over my snorkel. I had to clear it too often. I heard a voice, far away, a real voice. I lifted my head out of the water. I had reached the end of the isle and was facing the open sea. Looking to my right, I saw Matt on shore waving and shouting.

"We have to go. Everyone's looking for you. Turn around and swim back, you can't get out here."

I was too tired to question. I turned and started back. By the time I got there, the Zodiac had left for the main island. The Peruvians had another tour to meet. Matt was the only one there. We waited in the shallows until the Zodiak returned to pick us up. I don't remember any conversation on the ride back. I still felt confusion and amazement. Amazement that my son-in-law had run a mile and more in the midday, tropical sun to find and help me; amazed that I had swum over a mile. I can't swim, you see.

And where was my husband?

We reached the dock. I crawled out of the Zodiac. Terry was sitting at an umbrella-shaded table, sipping a Heineken, complaining that he had had to pay the tour guide an extra fare for making the trip back out for me. A worm deep in my gut began to shiver and spread. I felt sick, sitting on the dock, leaning against a pillar. I had wimped out, got lost, and cost time and money. I was not going to add throwing up on a public dock to my humiliation. I squeezed acupuncture points on the sides of my knees, squeezed until the nausea ebbed. I stood up and started to walk back to the Inn. The others followed. I finally had a voice. I turned to Terry and asked, "Weren't you worried? You know I'm afraid of water. You know I have no sense of direction. Weren't you worried? Why didn't you look for me? Why didn't you wait for me?"

He looked at me with hurt little-boy eyes and said, "Those turtles, those turtles were so cool!"

I said nothing. I just wanted to be alone again. I needed to get back to the inn, where I went straight to my room, rolled into a blanket. The worm was still shivering. The bed felt solid beneath me. I slept for hours.

Not much was ever said about the turtle tour. Several days later we went back to the Atlantic side of the island, the wild side. The sea rose close to the road there. Voodoo wards stood at intervals along the shore. We stopped and I walked respectfully out to photograph one. It was built of long pieces of driftwood balanced in a sort of offset teepee frame, with a shallow cairn of rocks supporting the base. A stick, standing off to one side had a doll tied to it. The main structure displayed a variety of sandals, old shoes, wooden spoons, and hand mixers, dangling in the wind. Standing next to the sacred shield, I felt the presence of the faith of the builders.

I knelt to get my picture, then looked up to watch the sea through the angles of wood and trinkets. I felt the builders' sense of trust. Trust that old sandals and red, plastic, measuring cups could hold back the fury of the sea. A faith and trust as unexplainable as fears that seem unfounded to those who don't fear. Trust breeds confidence. Confidence doesn't need logic to work. It doesn't even need reality. Confidence puts matter in the soul, strength to stand and say, "I can swim a mile, alone."

As I watched the Atlantic Ocean through a frame of voodoo, I knew a passage had slipped by, leaving something stronger in its wake.

She Who Casts in Trees

Terry and I were married in June at the height of trout season. Much to my family's amazement we gave each other fly fishing gear for wedding gifts. There were two sets of Ted McLean fly rods and automatic reels, nets, creels and rubber hip waders. The rods were eight feet long. I can leap many of our local native streams in a single bound; definitely overkill. Having never fished for trout before I tried my best to emulate pictures I had seen of people standing hip-deep in quiet streams with graceful halos of monofilament hovering above their heads. However, in spite of my most sincere efforts, from cast to cast my rod tip would end up in a tree on one shore and my fly in another across the stream. Meanwhile, Terry was meandering down-stream occasionally catching a fish with the gleeful shout, "Got another one"! After one such declaration, my Irish-Italian temper, which had been on a slow rise, boiled over and in a fit of frustration I pitched my rod into the water. Terry heard the splash and came sloshing back to find his bride sitting on a rock, fists clenched and a submerged fishing pole still attached to two trees. From that day forward, embellished versions of stories of Mom-fishing-in-trees have entertained family gatherings.

Our family friend Ed balances a white-frosted can of Dutchboy paint on the ladder, slanted against the porch roof. He waves away flies, hungry for a piece of sweaty flesh on this sultry August morning. "Hey, Rose, you wanna fish the tournament with me?"

I yank a dandelion, snapping its root. "The Tidioute tournament? I don't know, Ed, I have so much to do. I'm behind on these essays." Then I reconsider. "Ya know Ed, that would be fun. I haven't gone for years, don't have any equipment."

Ed smiles his quiet, close-lipped smile and asks, "Do you know how to throw for muskies?"

"Throw what?"

"Lures, like Rapalas. Have you ever cast them?"

Apparently fishing at Ed's level is going to entail a little vocabulary work up-front.

A few days later Ed shows up with a muskie pole, spinning reel and several Rapalas, hand crafted lures from Finland. Looking like a clutch of elongated Easter eggs, Rapalas come in a variety of sizes, colors and patterns designed to tease game fish into believing that they are tasty minnows or shiners. My favorite is a four-inch-long lovely called a slash-bait, with flashy colors, feathered tail and three sets of triple hooks.

Though I did some fresh water fishing when first married, with the advent of three children, fishing was one of the activities that fell by the wayside.

Its reintroduction three decades later came with the reintroduction of Ed into our lives. A consummate fisherman and talented chef, Ed had years earlier been my daughter Rachel's boyfriend. I had no issues with my daughters dallying with bad boys before settling down with a teacher, shopkeeper, electrician, whatever, as long as the finalist wasn't the outlaw. Ed was Rachel's bad boy. He once gave me a jumpsuit to wear while working with my bees. It is made of perfectly weighted olive green cotton, with an easy, zip-up front and the words Allegheny County Jail in yellow block letters across the back. Ed is a man with many stories.

We set up my rod, stand just off the porch steps and aim for the woods. Ed casts toward the pasture fence. Monofilament sings as it leaves the reel, arching gracefully and falling in silky waves to the ground. Lovely. My turn. I run through the steps in my head: two feet of line loose, shoulders flexed, snap tip at the end of throw. I cast, the line snakes to the ground, five feet in front me, a neat trick with a seven-foot pole! One factor short on my preflight checklist, I forgot to flip the bale, a little metal arch that flips from one side of the reel to the other, allowing the line to rewind or slip from the spool as needed. My second effort is greatly improved. With bale appropriately located, line cascades off the reel and zings from the tip of the pole, flying to the edge of the pasture fence, a bit to the right of target. Not bad, huh? Ed is a good teacher, patient and encouraging, especially encouraging.

I continue making good progress until my husband, Terry walks by, making jokes about hooks and branches. My thoughts tangle like a backlash in old insecurities. While Terry watches, I flub. When he goes to the barn my lure floats on air. Oh well.

At last the dry runs are over. We head for the river to try out the real thing. Terry hikes a quarter of a mile upriver, Ed moves downstream. I throw my creek chub. It's a nice heavy, segmented lure that swims well. No strikes. Over the period of an hour I go through my collection of lures with no success. In the bottom of my creel lies one more. Terry left his favorite Rapala, an 18cc shiner in my creel. I slip it out of the box, and snap it on a swivel. Fwitt, it sails across the current and retrieves like a real fish. I love it! This thing can catch fish! I throw again toward a deeper pool downstream. The line whips out, sails and flutters in loops to the water. Where's the end? Where's the plug? I look up and there, dangling 30 feet above my head, on an overhanging branch, is Terry's prize lure, a birthday gift from our son. I tug, wade out into the water, jerk, swing to the other side of the supporting deadfall, snap, swish, flail. Nothing. Irretrievable. The Ashbaugh family "tree caster" strikes again, after decades of dormancy.

Three weeks later we roll out of our driveway in the early, September chill. It's the first day of the Tidioute Fishing Tournament, and by 5a.m. I am in position where the tail waters spill over Kinzua Dam into the Allegheny River. The sky, a black, fleecy wrap around a barely full moon, fills with fog in the last hour before dawn. A cold, steady breeze rushes off the dam and rolls downstream.

Casting is difficult and the current is strong. My fingers grow wet and cold. I stand alone in the crisp, predawn dusk. As the dam releases its ghostly plumes of moonlit water, the roar pulses with the gusting wind. Absorbed in the throb of sound and mist, I cast and retrieve with no thought, lost in reverie, caught up in the sensation of a universal embrace. Minutes pass. Subtle hues leak through the clouds adding streaks of pink and orange to the graying darkness. As the sun rises I see through to the streambed and venture out in the current. A bald eagle tacks into the stiff breeze and circles the dam, searching for breakfast.

Visible in the early light, a thick layer of foam floats to several feet off the bank. The day brightens and a school of fish push their gulping lips through the foam, skimming for food. I switch to a smaller lure and cast into the foam. I feel a bump on each cast but no strike.

By 9 o'clock the men show up, hungry for breakfast. I just want a hot cup of coffee to hold in my numb fingers.

The rest of the day we move from hole to hole, rotating lures according to the waters and their suspected inhabitants. At times, when Ed calls "Let's move," I find it hard to pull out. Fishermen don't quit. In my mind I hear Billy Joel's "Downeaster Alexa", a ballad about a bait fisherman who mortgages his house to keep his boat and continue fishing rather than lose it to a factory job.

So if you see my Downeaster Alexa
And if you work with the rod and the reel
Tell my wife I am trolling Atlantis
And I still have hands on the wheel.

We climb down steep banks, clutching branches and rocks as we seek a good hole of hungry fish. We meet polite boaters, friendly fellow fishers and a lonely old man whose arthritis keeps him off the water, but doesn't prevent him from watching others.

By 4:30 we have wandered 40 miles downstream, much of it in the comfort of Terry's pickup truck. We share the Tionesta bridge with a few off-shore fishermen in boats. I'm delighted to see that I can now cast into some of the same holes the boaters use. This is it. If we don't catch anything here we don't qualify for the fish-off tomorrow. After an hour the guys reel in their tackle and start up the hill to our cars.

"One more throw," I mutter. One more moment of optimistic hope, like one last quarter in the slot machine. I work my best Rapala Huskie. In the Internet chat room everyone said this was a sure catcher in evening waters. It swam its little heart out for me, dipping and swerving like a wounded minnie. No hits. No fish. Time for supper.

I dry my hopeful little lure and smooth its feathered tail. Smiling, I recall the poignant humor of the great blues lyricist David Lee Murphy:

If the fish ain't bitin'
If the fish ain't bitin'
Well now don't go gettin' shook
Honey take a look
What kinda bait you got on the hook

Ed apologizes for not finding a "hot" hole for me, and I try to tell him I don't care. I had a wonderful day, the finest that I've had in a while. It's not about the fish for me. It's about life and freedom and serenity. It's about the eagle that flies at dawn, the river water that embraces my legs, the trees that whisper secrets through their leaves. Ed's eyes swipe across mine. He turns and rests his ebony muskie pole on his shoulder.

We walk along a gravel access road to the parking lot. Ed's Bass Pro cap is tilted up and there's a slight swagger in his step. He says, "Ya know, Rose, we oughtta buy a boat. That would get us out to the good holes. Yep, we oughtta buy a boat."

Brown Betty

They bought a boat this October, my husband and his fish-frenzied pal, Ed. It's a twelve-foot, Feathercraft, one of the first aluminum fishing boats, made in the 1950's. Ed found it in a neighbor's front yard with a For Sale sign propped against the keel. Terry brought it home in the bed of his weathered Toyota pickup truck. They seemed well matched, the boat and the truck. I helped Terry lift it down and carry it into the barn. We set it in the middle of the floor. Like a squat chameleon, it faded into the dust, webs and hay, scattered on the worn wooden planks. We didn't have much to say. I went back to winterizing my flower gardens. Terry slid the barn doors closed and disappeared into that portal-to-another-universe that I'm convinced is hidden in our garage.

We awakened the next morning to scraping sounds emanating from the barn, Ed's Ford Festiva parked in front. For weeks the barn buzzed, screeched, leaked halogen rays at night, as if an alien fetus incubated in its bowels. Like high school prom queens selecting the perfect gown and just-right accessories, Terry and Ed spent hours on the Internet, deciding on paint, oars and a motor.

She debuted on a bright Saturday afternoon as my golden retriever, Sophie, and I returned from a walk. Terry met us at the edge of the woods. He asked, with the caution bred of 38 years navigating the shifting currents of a relationship, "Um, wanna see the boat?"

"Sure," I chirped and we stepped into the barn.

She sat, propped upright, the shiny color of milk chocolate just before it melts. Her lipstick red, vinyl, swivel seats perched bow and stern of center. A bark-camo Briggs and Stratton motor tilted on its mount. Glazed black and silver registration numbers aligned perfectly along her forward gunnels, a set of high gloss maple oars dangling from the locks. Sophie sniffed the circumference, cautiously at first, then in tail-wagging delight. I dittoed Sophie's approval. This transformation boded well for years of fun and adventure. I enjoyed dancing images of summer days drifting along quiet waters and introducing my grandson to the addiction of plying the rod and the reel.

"Ya done good guys!" I said. "This is gonna be fun."

With a can of Yuengling lager, Terry christened her Brown Betty. We launched her with the sunrise on Pymatuning Lake, near Linesville. Betty could only hold two of us at a time so we spent the day in a wolf-cabbage-goat conundrum reenactment. I spent the morning wading off shore. Ed chose an island for the afternoon lull. Terry worked the evening shift on shore, while Ed and I motored out to the Stump Field.

The Pymatuning Stump Field is a shallow area where masses of ghostly limbs beckon from the surface, concealing tangled branches that lurk below. Pan fish, rock bass, perch, and potential meals of Cajun catfish hang out in the submerged maze of roots and boughs. Ed and I approached with caution and dropped anchor a long, cast length from the largest tangle.

Evening advanced and so did fishy appetites and fortunately we pulled in a feisty mess of nice fish for supper. On one strike a fish took Ed's line into an underwater den, tangling his setup hopelessly. Unfortunately Ed's favorite steelhead bobber, a weighted, mini-foo jig from Alaska, wss attached. Ed struggled and we nudged Betty closer but to no avail. Ed finally cut the line.

"Watch for it," he said.

In seconds the bobber shot to the surface and snagged on a twig. "I think we can get it before we leave," Ed hoped out loud.

We fished until darkness loomed. Ed reved the motor and started for an open channel. I shouted back, "What about that bobber?"

Ed smacked his forehead and spun Betty in a tight arc around the far side of the stumps. He cut the motor and we drifted in with a sudden, bump stop. "Uh-oh," breathed Ed.

I tried to reach out but we were several feet shy of goal. Ed rowed with one oar. Ed pulled hard. We gained some inches. When he paddled off starboard we sank back; gain three, loose two, gain three, lose two. Ed was working up a pretty good sweat. Finally he muttered, "I better do this the right way. Even if it scrapes, it's getting dark, we gotta get off." He sat down, placed the oars in the locks and began to row. Finally he held ground, inching forward, straining against the pull.

Then, "Rose?" Ed grunted.

I looked over my shoulder at his sweat-glazed face, and responded, "Huh?"

"You did pull the anchor?" he asked.

Our eyes met in an "oh shit!" moment.

With the damp rope of the anchor coiled against my leg we headed back to the dock where Terry was waiting with the truck. The cackle from a wedge of passing Canada geese receded along the narrow corridor of Pymatuning lake.

Fish Story

Wings spread in threatening array, two Peking ducks squabble over a chunk of stale Italian bread. "Think they're mine, Daddy?" the girl muses. The early afternoon sun lights her face. They sit on a red plaid stadium blanket at the pond's edge; yellow spadderdock lilies bob along the shoreline. Tiny insect surfers ride sun laced ripples that shimmer across the surface. She leans against him, into his warmth, content in the shadow of her hero, taking him for granted. She didn't know then that heroes grow old and die.

Five years old, and in love with all things furry, I was captivated by the fuzzy, yellow ducklings huddled in a wire pen at Murphy's Five and Ten. Dad squatted at a nearby counter, studying egg dying kits. By the time we checked out, he had a sack of color tablets with wire egg holders and I had a shoebox with pencil holes punched in the lid, my first Easter duckling.

By the year of my fifth duck, Dad and I had a system. About a week before Easter, he arrived home with the telltale shoebox. I arranged a large cardboard carton with a dangling light bulb and torn rags. The bird hungrily gobbled a warm, grainy-smelling gruel that I mixed for him. Food splattered off his orange bill. In the evening I cuddled with him in my overstuffed TV chair. His feathers soft as I held him, stroked his head. His eyes drifted shut. He fluffed asleep in my reassuring hand.

By Memorial Day, the duck could no longer be confined in his box; stiff white feathers already replaced the yellow fuzz. Time for father and daughter to make their annual trip to the Homewood Cemetery.

On oue hands and knees, Dad and I would clear the brush in front of a small stone that read Leah Kennevan – his mother's grave.

When we had finished planting marigolds around the granite marker, we walked to the duck pond, a restful haven just beyond the chapel. There, I released my pet and he waddled off to find a real duck family.

As we sat by the pond, I dangled a line off a spool of kite string, a tiny, gold hook tied to the end. We dipped stale bread in water and shaped it into a ball around the hook. Little sunfish bumped the bait and occasionally one would, greedily, swallow it whole. After I lifted the flapping fish on shore, Dad, with huge, meaty hands smoothed the dorsal fin and deftly pried the hook from the gaping mouth. While Dad's fingers worked, the fish would kaleidoscope through a range of hues; green, yellow, orange, blue, until it was finally free to flick its tail and disappear into the depths of the pond. As hours drifted by like minutes, the new duck persistently quacked and insisted his way into the flock and we sat there in the warming sun, below Leah's grave, Dad and I and the orphan ducks, a family reunion.

Five decades later, one October morning on Wookcock Creek Lake, this childhood scene appears in my mind. Perhaps it's the fishing, the droning hum of our trolling motor, the vibration, the grey cape of fog around our boat. Draped in a tan, fleece poncho, I stare mindlessly at the tip of my pole. Hypnotic. A chill inhale brings me to the shivering reality of this foggy lake, one of the top ten muskie waters in Pennsylvania. Wispy pillars of fog, gypsy ghost dancers, slip away as we approach. Here and there a cluster pirouettes, rising to the brooding clouds. My husband, Terry, and I troll the far shore of Wookcock, from the dam embankment to the creek source. The fog thins. An isolated residence takes shape. Lights warm the windows. Perhaps the owners, wrapped in sleep-warmed sheets, drift through a lazy Sunday morning.

Something hits Terry's bait! He cuts the motor. I reel in quickly to give him room. A young muskie breeches, brave enough to be fun and small enough to guarantee his release. As Terry lifts him onboard, his scales shimmer, mossy stripes darkening. A memory snags as I watch Terry's thick, strong fingers wrestling with the treble hooks caught up in the muskie's gills. I bundle deeper into my poncho and drift away.

Bill Kennevan was born to be the father of sons. Instead he had my sister and me. He didn't seem to care. Dad was a champion of women's rights. He never told us that we couldn't do something because we were girls. His only rule was, "Never quit. If you start it, finish it."

Although a real estate broker who worked long hours every day, Dad gave me a half-day a week; Wednesdays usually. We visited planetariums, train shows, made and flew kites, and we fished. When we began to vacation at the Jersey shore, Dad and I went off in rented boats, fishing larger waters now.

He started me off on party boats, where 16 to 20 people stood shoulder-to-shoulder around the railings. When our favorite skipper, Captain Cramer, found the right spot, we would all drop our lines in and hope our bait would be the chosen one. Occasionally, a lucky fisherman would catch a sea bass or flounder. Usually we caught nasty-looking denizens called sea robins, bottom dwellers with razor sharp spines and broad, slimy heads. Sometimes a shark would hit the tasty string of squid and bloodworms sucking up lines on one side of the boat, diving under and hitting those on the other side. Captain Cramer, shedding his usual jolly composure, frantically cut the lines, losing a day's profits in the tangled string of tackle, trailing a sated shark.

When I could go the distance on a party boat, could avoid throwing up and seemed to sincerely enjoy the experience, we began to charter. Usually we ran for bonito. On one trip I caught a dolphin. Not the aquatic mammal variety, but a true fish, the one caught by Hemingway's Santiago, who ate it raw for the strength to land his marlin.

Known in Hawaii as a Mahi-Mahi, the dolphin fish, colored like a giant form of my old duck-pond sunfish, flies a sickle shaped tail and sweeping dorsal fin. Mine was four feet long and fought for over twenty minutes, the strongest fish I have ever confronted. I released him back into the Atlantic.

Dad loved Hemingway and particularly admired Santiago because the old man refused to give up, even when sharks attacked his fish. Sitting astern, in our cushioned, swivel chairs, poles riding angled in outriggers, we trolled off the Jersey shore, beyond sight of land. We talked about going south some year to run for blue marlin. We might catch a monster like Santiago. We never made it. Dad ran out of time.

The hazy morning on Woodcock Creek Lake gives way to cold patches of sunlight. A bank of cumulus clouds rolls, a cresting wave looming over the lake. The needling wind works its way through my poncho. By lunchtime, I shiver uncontrollably, chilled to the bone. We beach the boat. I start the truck and huddle in front of the heater, wolfing my turkey sandwich like a starving refugee. I choose to take the next shift on shore.

The midday score has Terry with two muskie, caught from the boat, Ed with three, hooked while fishing off shore, and me with several feisty patches of seaweed.

As the men motor off toward the dam, I find I am more comfortable on shore where I can move and shelter from the wind. With the third cast I land a 16 inch, small mouth bass. Nice fish. He fights well. A clean hook, he is easy to release. Then, the mother-of-all crayfish hits my worm. I plop him on shore. He hangs on, with one large claw grasping the line, as his smaller, feeder pinchers rip off chunks of worm. The second large claw waves, menacingly, in my direction. I dip him in the water. He hangs on. I smack him on the surface. He continues gobbling tasty, wormy chunks. I cast the line out and reel it back in again. There he is. With gloved fingers, I slip the worm off the hook and leave the crustacean to his lunch in a shallow pool between some partially submerged rocks.

As is our pattern, Ed and I take the evening shift in the boat. Sun breaks steadily through the clouds now and the wind has died. We decide to troll a deep channel down the middle of Woodcock. Ed catches a nice muskie, number eight for the day, none large enough to keep. Meanwhile I have a bass, seaweed and the mother of all crayfish on my side. Ed says, "We have to get you a fish." I think, "So what's a bass?"

We make pass after pass. No more hits. Tired, cold and hungry, I call Terry on the walkie-talkie to say that we'll make one more turn and put in at the launch. Yards from the last turn my pole snaps into a dangerous arc. I have a snag. My lure is nailed to the bottom. Ed cuts the motor. I reel. Ed says, "That line's coming in. You have a fish!"

I pull, wrestle the tip up, ease the drag, careful to allow no slack, still hearing Dad's quiet coaching from so long ago, "Calm, steady pressure, let him play himself out." Finally, he breeches, a tiger muskie, rolling and dancing, fighting with all the tricks nature gave him. I bring him alongside. Ed is so excited that his hands shake as he works the net. The fish measures 30 and ¾ inches. He's legal. I slip a stringer through his gill slit and lower him into the water. He tries to pull away, jolting the boat. I just want a picture and bragging rights. I only caught one, but mine was the biggest by far. We have our photo session and hugs around. The men are delighted

I wade back into the water. As I pump the sluggish muskie by his tail, side to side, then forward and backward, forcing water through the gills, he revives. He nudges forward, no dramatic splash and charge. With a slight pulse of his caudal fin he is gone. Gone, as the past is gone, leaving his residue in memory.

Elderberry Wine

In early June my grandfather Joe used to find elderberry blossoms in full bloom and cut them for elderberry blossom wine. The summer of our births he set aside a bottle of elderberry blossom wine each, for my sister and me. The wine was to be opened on the day of our weddings. He died when I was fifteen. On my wedding day we opened the last bottle of Grandpap Joe's elderberry blossom wine. It was twenty-four years old, clear amber and lightly fruity. We used it to toast the end of an era, the end of childhood.

> *"There should be a song for women to sing at this moment, or a prayer to recite. But perhaps there is none because there are no words strong enough to name that moment. Like every mother since the first mother, I was overcome and bereft, exalted and ravaged. I have crossed over from girlhood. I beheld myself as an infant in my mother's arms, and caught a glimpse of my own death. I wept, without knowing whether I rejoiced or mourned. My mothers and their mothers were with me as I held my baby."*
>
> *~ from The Red Tent by Anita Diamant*

My sister Gigi and I exchanged happy messages through the winter of 2004, as her youngest son and his wife, Tara, and my youngest daughter and her husband,

Eric, were expecting babies one month apart. Gigi was an experienced grandmother by now but I was in my novitiate. We knew Neely's baby was a boy and his name would be Jacob Owen. Craig and Tara wanted to be surprised. Since Gigi is an avid wine maker I suggested that if Tara and Craig had a girl she could revive grandpap Joe's tradition of putting up a bottle of elderberry blossom wine the summer of a girl-child's birth.

Terry and I joined the ranks of expectant grandparents, navigating the aisles of Babies r Us and Toys r Us, two retired teachers wondering at having educated a generation of dyslexic merchants. We also began reading. We scanned volumes on fetal development and pored over Neely's emailed sonograms. We wondered how we managed our own pregnancies in a state of developmental ignorance, not to mention the Kools, Bacardi and Cokes, and unpasteurized cheese. Miraculously, our children grew up in spite of us and we wished the same good fortune for them as parents.

My head fell back on the crispy, sanitized pillow, eyes roaming over the bold-faced clock, high on the delivery room wall. Somewhere close to midnight. A frantic piece of my mind whimpered, *I don't think I can do this.* The thought must have slipped out of my mind and into the delivery room. An accommodating anesthesiologist offered a rubber mask and the ribbed tube slid over my shoulder. I heard a woman's voice say, "You're almost there."

I knew the voice, the funny one. That summer everyone was reading *Rosemary's Baby,* a thriller about the birth of the Antichrist. The funny nurse teased since I hit the labor room.

"Hey guys, this is Rosemary. Hope her baby doesn't come on our shift."

"Yikes, she's eight centimeters dilated. Call the exorcist!"

I pushed the mask away, growled out pushes like a woman possessed then fell back to that fucking crispy pillow.

In the late 60s in rural, northwestern Pennsylvania the local obstetric community had not caught on to the current trend of having fathers in the delivery room. After months of determined badgering, Dr. Turbessi promised that Terry could stay in the labor room with me until the last moments when I would have to go alone into "delivery."

We planned this together, Terry and I. There were no natural childbirth classes in our community. We spent months with our yellow Lamaze natural childbirth book, doing the exercises and practicing puffy breaths on the trailer floor. Terry coached. Each day, I stood by the kitchen window watching the Allegheny River flow south to Pittsburgh, practiced relaxation drills, and the muscle strengthening, "pelvic rock." I preferred exercising outside but the "pelvic rock" was getting too much attention from our elderly, next-door neighbor and passing motorists. By this late August afternoon we were armed and ready to deliver our drug-free baby.

My labor progressed well. And then at this critical point, they separated us. I tilted my head up, backwards on the gurney and watched an upside down Terry drift out of sight at the end of the corridor, as rubber-treaded wheels rumbled on the tile floor. With a bump the double doors swung inward to a chilly, bright-white room.

I panted like a sweaty sprinter. Waves of contractions tightened, pushed down. I sank into the pressure. I heard my voice deep in my chest, humming with the throaty tones of a didgeridoo. I was the moon tilting on her axis, sister to generations in caves, in huts and mansions, a rhythm I never heard until this moment sounded through my body. Some urgent voices shouted, "Push! Push!" My body curled like a caterpillar around a twig as every muscle pulled together. With a warm gush, the head slipped out. I felt the baby rotate. I didn't know if it was a boy or girl. It was breathing and crying. I was squeezing the shit out of somebody's fingers. One more easy push and there he was, a red-slimed, wrinkled, crooked-headed baby boy. He was so beautiful, I couldn't stop looking at him as a nurse took him away to clean, weigh and measure him. The funny nurse stage whispered, "Stick a bonnet over those horns before the mother sees them."

From his first cuddly moments, Ian was a bright-eyed creature in love with life. His cries never had the fierce fury we would hear from his little sister three years later.

Ian was born thirty days after Neil Armstrong walked on the moon. The TV bracketed to the wall of my hospital room replayed his "One step for mankind . . ." mini speech. That may have been the ultimate moment for you, Neil, I thought, but you will never experience what I just did.

Through Ian's early years, his parents were busy opposing the war in Vietnam, the Nixon administration and segregation. We dressed him in miniature army fatigues with embroidered peace signs. We took him to rock concerts, where he toddled through clouds of reefer smoke. His thick, platinum hair grew long and shaggy. Who would have guessed that one day this hippy love-child would grow up to become a pharmacist, a businessman, a short-haired, briefcase-carrying conservative?

It happens in the best of families.

On the morning of the last day of June, I received an email from my sister titled "Sad News". *There is no easy way to say this. Tara and Craig lost the baby today.* The baby was beautiful, a perfect 7 pound 13 ounce little girl with blond hair. They named her Ella Louise. A section of the umbilical cord had thinned and kinked when she rolled, cutting off her blood supply. It happened the day before her due date, robbing her of the chance to gulp in this world and scream it out, taste it and revel in it with a baby's abandon.

It was so difficult to express sympathy over two thousand miles of continent. We established a section of children's books on grieving in Ella's name in their neighborhood library. It was a gesture but not a hug. A year passed before we met face-to-face.

Ella's shadow drifted over the final weeks of Neely's pregnancy. During those days I felt the need to narrow my focus, hold tight, stay on course. For a month we all kept an eye to shore and steadfastly rode the current to the day of Jacob's birth.

When the call finally came from Neely we loaded already packed suitcases into the 4Runner, notified the neighbor children to look after the pets and headed south. My daughter welcomed us all into the delivery room, her parents, grandmother, sister, Eric's parents, seven in all. Our voices joined the midwife in a countdown with each contraction. Cheers and helpful words of encouragement accompanied every push, every centimeter of progress. We described the mass of thick dark hair on his emerging head as if we were art students in a museum. A room humming with excitement, joy and relief greeted Jacob Owen's first lusty squall of life, a room that held souls from ninety years to ninety seconds old.

When we finally gave parents and child their well deserved private time, darkness had fallen. We drove back to Neely's house to care for their hungry cats.

I helped Mom into the living room and went back out for my backpack. I stood by the car and gazed up at the night sky. A bright messenger streaked passed the Pleiades, heralding the approach of the Perseids meteor shower. The Big Dipper seemed to hang on a celestial peg in the western sky as if it held in its bowl the chorus of toads and tree frogs who entertained the night prowlers. Standing in this massive amphitheater, I thought of Ella, the cousin Jacob will never know.

We have an old barn on our land in Tidioute. It was originally a stable for the carriages and horses. A gabled roof tops walls of silvered barn board. On the pasture side, sheltered from the road, an unruly colony of elderberry bushes grows. Palm-sized clusters of feathery white flowers bloom in early summer. As the dew dries in late morning, a few honeybees stop by to test the nectar flow. They return to the hive with information of sticky, golden pools, and the labor force swells through the day, bees darting in and out, working intensely at tiny, lacy flowers, extracting nectar and seeding next year's bloom. Only as the evening cools with the setting sun does their number dwindle until the last worker abandons her duties for the night.

When bees have full bellies and nothing to fear, I enjoy working among them in my Allegheny County Jail suit. Their ceaseless hum dampens the noisy clutter of life and provides a time of peace. In the fall, when the elderberry blossoms ripen into drooping bunches of indigo berries, the bees work Queen Ann's lace and wild asters. I blend into the environment, careful to avoid their flight paths, and gingerly snip thin arching branches laden with berries into a plastic garbage bag. I freeze them, making it easy to shake the dark berries into my jelly pot with few of the tiny stems falling in.

Two years after Jacob's birth, Neely had a little girl. In this first June of Madeline Rose's life I went among the bees and gathered flowers for a new bottle of elderberry blossom wine.

Aging Warriors

This story begins with a lanky, fourteen-year old girl, sporting brown, curly hair, in a boyish cut. She stands on a busy Pittsburgh street corner waiting for the 73 Highland trolley. She wears a pleated, blue-green watch plaid skirt, crisp white shirt and navy vest, with the gold emblem of Sacred Heart High School embroidered on the breast. She slouches, hip cocked to one side to help support an armload of texts and notebooks. A large man, six feet tall and twice her breadth quietly slips up behind her. He shouts and grabs her by the shoulders. The girl springs out of her slouch, rotates, slamming her elbow into the man's temple, knocking him to the sidewalk. Pedestrians stop walking. Others turn toward the scene. The man's black satchel, full of medical supplies and equipment, skitters off the sidewalk, into the gutter.

The girl stands, fists clenched, books and papers scattered and blowing across the sidewalk. She stares incredulously at her beloved family doctor, in his immaculate gray suit, sprawled on the ground. "Dr. Rylands!" she mutters, in shock. Then, voice rising, "You scared me. Oh, I'm so sorry. I'm so sorry," she repeats over and over helping him to his feet. Someone retrieves his medical bag. A few other students gather the girl's books and papers.

"Don't be sorry, Rosie," he laughs. "I deserved what I got. Your parents never have to worry about you taking care of yourself." From that day on my medical bills arrived addressed to "Slugger Kennevan".

That old story is very important to me. I reach back to it when I need a confidence boost. I'm not a gifted athlete and as a child was always the last one sitting on the bench. But when I need strength–emotional as well as physical–I find it, and I've learned, in decades of martial arts study, to call it *ch'i*.

"My butt's numb, mom, I can't drive any longer!"

My son's baritone voice startles me out of a travel-induced hypnosis and snaps me back to the real world of our six-hour drive to Philadelphia. Ian has been planning this trip for months. It is a rare opportunity for us, and our martial arts teacher, Handest Sensei, to study with a sword master from California. Master McLean conducts seminars in cutting with live blade katana. We have been working with two of the thirty-six inch long, Samurai swords since Christmas time and feel ready for more advanced instruction.

My two-month old SUV still smells of new-car, mixed with a blend of wet retriever, lingering on a forgotten dog blanket bunched in the cargo net, ripening fruit and bar-b-q soy chips. Sensei is in the back seat surrounded by swords and hakamas, skirted uniforms worn by sword handlers. He is imitating the voice of my navigational device. He likes to say that it is difficult to tell the difference between a Zen master and a lunatic. We smile and agree.

What am I doing out here again, going off to play with boys? It was easy when I was young and flexible and healed fast. Now, at sixty-one, it seems an unnecessary risk. Someone's going to hurt me. They always do. Either hurt or ignore me. Since I can't tolerate being ignored, I'll engage them, make them know I'm someone to be reckoned with. Then they'll hurt me. But I never let it show. That's getting harder too. It's difficult enough being a girl who plays with boys, but an old girl who plays with boys has a rough row to hoe. If only I liked knitting, got some sort of satisfaction from maintaining a clean house or watching soaps. None of that does it for me. I like men. I like their uncluttered, "what you see is what you get" style. They play fun games with fun toys, like swords that can remove a man's head and shoulder with one strike. But they're also strong, fast and can hurt.

My history with the martial arts is linked to our family commitment to foster care. The experience slipped into our lives with the quiet urging of two teachers to "do something" about the number of badly parented kids and ended with Kenny, the last of twenty seven adolescents to merge in and out of out of our lives. Ken has remained a permanent member of the clan as well as the martial arts school.

Life in a foster home can seem dauntingly crowded, for parents as well as their biological kids. We tried to support their interests and spend time with them. I played racket ball with Ian weekly. In 1987 Rachel decided that she would like to study karate. I had two colleagues who studied in a traditional dojo, a Japanese term commonly used for the place where karate is studied. With their encouragement we joined and Ian and Neely followed us in time. Over two decades later the art remains an integral part of our lives.

The training area at Shuto Society Dojo is a bright, spacious room with two lengths of windows along the outside walls. Swords, boken, wooden training swords, and mats line the floor. Our host, Robinson Sensei, greets us at the entrance with a gentle air of authority. His twelve, barefoot, hakama-clad students are delightfully friendly and relaxed as they welcome our rag-tag little band of three.

Master McLean is already on the floor, ready to begin the six-hour training session. He is a solidly built Celt, half Welsh, half Scottish, his dark, curly hair and beard, graying with his fifth decade. He wears a black hackama with matching kimono top, sleeves tied up Samurai style, with a multicolored rope. The effect is to further broaden his shoulders and accentuate his fluid movements. He is a skilled teacher.

Because our levels are unknown to Master McLean, we join the empty-hand group; these are the students who practice the skills required before taking a weapon in hand. This is exactly the discipline we hoped for. At home all three of us are teachers. In our school the title of sensei is earned with promotion to the rank of second-degree black belt. Here, we enjoy the role of student.

The drills are exhausting, challenging and progress relentlessly. I don't catch on. Hours go by. I work with the other slower ones. Ian comes forward to be my partner. I don't have to be guarded with him. I can wallow in my ineptitude and self-pity. He says, "Your eyes are getting bright, mom. What's wrong?" From the time he was three he has always known when I was sad. He would touch me with his little hands and say, "What's wrong, mommy?" Once, in confused frustration, he asked, "What does it take to make you happy, mom?"

One thing that makes me happy, now, is stepping out of easy security and into challenge. I've been around long enough to be comfortable with the knowledge that it's okay not to be number one; that the real treasures are unearthed in the sandy plains and tangled jungles of our struggles, like bravely walking into Master McLean's sword seminar and taking my place in the line of students.

In our sixth decade my husband Terry and I are dealing with an emerging role-reversal situation. That is, our adult children are beginning to doubt our competency. They're critical of what we watch and eat, check expiration dates on food and meds and look unduly concerned over what we think are hilarious "senior moment" stories. Combined with our obviously failing bodies and memories, their attitudes begin to erode our confidence.

All I can say is, they better not come up behind me unexpectedly, or they might find Slugger Kennevan alive and well.

Drive-Time Italian

"C'e una macchina nuova." *There is a new car,* Antonio states cheerfully.

"Si, c'e una macchina." *Yes there is a car,* Ester agrees.

As I swing the 4Runner into my driveway, I'm startled to find myself home, and realize that I have daydreamed through three lessons of "Drive Time Italian." I slide the CD out as the Pioneer navigational unit glides into a recessed slot. Reluctantly I leave the warmth of the car and enter a night chill that bites through my fleece jacket. I inhale dry, cold air and stand spellbound, watching as the Dipper balances impossibly on the tip of its handle while Orion tumbles wildly, over the barn roof. Cirque du Soleil in the night sky.

Shouldering my bags I sidle through the entry door. Under-cabinet lighting wraps the corridor of our kitchen in a warm glow. The room still smells hungrily of the something-with-onions-and-peppers that Terry cooked for dinner. In the living room CNN headline news reports new war casualties, as the dogs belatedly announce that security has been breeched. I remind them that I live here and their barks transform into tail slapping grovels. A round, yellow, cow-jumped-over-the-moon cookie jar grins a friendly greeting from the top shelf of a glass cabinet.

After dad died in 1987, Mom moved in with us and brought many of the old things with her, the cookie jar among them. It is an antique now; my daughter, Neely, found one like it in a shop for $115.00. It used to sit in the middle of the kitchen table in the house on Glenview. It was one of the places that my grandfather would hide what I called my "card bars." Wednesday night was his pinochle night. With his winnings, or what was left of his stake, he would buy a Hershey bar and hide it somewhere in the kitchen or dining room for me. He never said a word about it and neither did I. It was our little game.

On rainy days, Cathy Pelligrino, my best of all friends, and I would sit at the rectangular steel-and-chrome kitchen table for hours playing Old Maid and War, helping ourselves to Nonie's cookies. The cookie jar's smiling moon face shone, a cheery kibbutzer, watching our games. From time to time I would grasp the leaping cow that served as a handle on the lid and quietly open the jar. If Nonie missed hearing the soft bisque scrape of the lid we each helped ourselves to another cookie.

Cathy was a year younger and a head shorter, my only female friend. Her thick hair fell to her waist, the color of melted chocolate chips. Her perpetually melancholy expression was deepened by inscrutable brown eyes. Her parents were from Sicily. Theirs was an arranged marriage; Virginia was five or so years older than Mike, who had been a sculptor in the Old Country. However, there wasn't much need for statuary in a 1950's steel town so Mike learned to apply his artistry to laying brick and stone.

I could watch him for hours, building a wall or walkway, listening to the scrape of his trowel as he scooped just the right amount of mortar, plopped it onto the brick and deftly spread, smoothed and sliced the excess away with the powerful, rhythmic movements of a flamenco dancer. At night Mike disappeared into his basement studio where we heard mysterious sounds and singing. Against her parents' rules, Cathy and I sneaked down once. Shelves lined the walls. They were crowded with busts of Mary and Jesus. There were colorful statues of the Infant of Prague and stacks of crucifixes. It was dark and eerie and a little sad.

Back out on the street I played hide and seek with Cathy and our gang of friends. In the yards and alleyways of our neighborhood, at least six dialects of Italian rang in my ears, mixed with Yiddish from the other side of the street and a symphony of European accents that enriched the speech of the Jewish elders who brought an extraordinary texture to the neighborhood. On this block long, dead-end street lived classical musicians, linguists, doctors and college professors, some in various stages of transferring their credentials to Pennsylvania regulations.

My parents expected my sister Gigi and me to take school just as seriously. Homework was structured and supervised and unavoidable. As a small child, I watched my sister surrounded by math texts, graphs and stacks of paper and through the windows across the street, saw older kids helping younger siblings and entire families sitting around the table, working together. When I was old enough to be part of the working crowd, my father checked my every paper, project, and quiz. He stressed education as the only path to success. He said that Irish Catholics had to work twice as hard to be considered half as good. It was a given that we would attend college and life would be better for us.

Perhaps this is why, five decades later, I am exchanging *arrivedercis, ciaos* and *pregos* with Antonio and Ester of *Drive-Time Italian.* If only I could exchange them with Cathy's father, as well. It probably also helps to explain how my sister's decision to attend her fiftieth college reunion a few years ago ended in my enrolling in a master's program in creative writing. And how, somewhere in the midst of that, I signed up to learn Chinese.

Caller ID read ALBERTA, announcing my only sibling 's weekly call home from Canada. I hit the talk button and said "Hi Gi." My follow-up "How are you?" question was cut off at the "How."

"I got an invitation for my 50th reunion at Carlow. It's in October, I know you're back to work then, but I'd like to come down for it. We can go together. I'll send the form and schedule."

In disbelief, I heard myself saying, "Sure, send me the stuff. Here, I'll get you over to Mom."

I handed the phone to Mom, irritated with myself for agreeing so easily. I hate reunions. Then I considered the fact that this was the first thing my big sister had ever asked me to do for her. My mother's joy as Gigi told her that she would be coming home in October further eased my frustration.

Phone calls and forms meandered from Edmonton to Tidioute to Pittsburgh. We chose our events and settled on a Saturday morning writers' workshop for our first activity.

On a drizzly October day we set off on an adventure both into our past and toward the future. In two hours our tires were churning wetly across the slick asphalt of rout 279, heading toward town, Pittsburgh, toward home. That magnificent skyline, dressed in a filmy robe of mist, stretched long and tall. She reached out to embrace her prodigal daughters.

The challenge of finding a parking spot at Carlow University on a rainy day hadn't improved since my graduation, 38 years earlier, when the institution was called Mount Mercy College. We finally found a spot large enough to accommodate my pickup truck. On foot, we finessed a diagonal cut across Fifth Avenue through the now driving rain. We dripped our way into a workshop taught by Pat Dobler. The written exercises she led us through must have lured out my repressed ambition to write a family story, because when she announced at the end of the class that Carlow would inaugurate an MFA program in writing in little over a year, I decided then and there to apply.

A year later, the excitement of acceptance into the program washed over my family then ebbed into the startling realization that I was going back to school! I had just retired from a thirty-three year career as a public school speech therapist, into a delightful three day-a-week position in a private preschool. Life was supposed to get easier. Three decades ago I finished my master's degree in speech and language. Other than yearly in-service trainings, I hadn't been in a classroom since. Could I still learn?

Sheer perversity led me to make sure by pitching myself headfirst into yet another educational experience.

One evening in May, I saw a flier posted in our local coffee shop announcing that a young friend who had been studying in China for several years was home and offering a summer class in Mandarin. "Okay," I thought. "If I can learn Mandarin, I can learn anything," and enrolled for the summer session.

Paul Goodwill, or Teacher Paul, as we called him, held class on Tuesday and Thursday evenings in his father's furniture store. Comfortably settled on couches, recliners and around wooden dining room tables, a diverse group plowed through an incomprehensible language. We struggled with impossibly subtle intonations, vocabulary with no Latin root for clues and written characters that were more art than alphabet. The class members ranged from college students considering foreign study, to older travelers planning trips, to the mother of an adopted Asian child and a cluster of local Tai Chi practitioners.

Teacher Paul began each session with a quiz, in Mandarin. He attempted to engage us in brief conversational exchanges. We laughed a lot and, with Paul's sunny, patient smile and constant encouragement we learned. Eventually I gained enough courage to say *xie xie,* or thank you, to the wait-staff in our local Chinese restaurant. They grinned largely. But they didn't laugh, so I left hefty tips.

By January, when my first MFA residency at Carlow arrived on the calendar I was ready to drive off to Pittsburgh, leaving Terry and Mom on their own for eleven days. I had my backpack, my camera and a new Powerbook that Terry had given me for my birthday. And so it began, and before I knew it, I had two semesters and a dozen personal essays under my belt.

And then, as the MFA program moved into its second year, for no apparently sane reason, I chose to finally do something about the fact that I could not speak Italian. Which takes us back to the driveway where we began.

"C'e una macchina nuova." *There is a new car,* says Antonio, his patience never wearing thin.

"Si, c'e una macchina." *Yes there is a car,* Ester agrees.

And I, too, agree. There is a car.

A Touch of Early Frost

Barb Swanson and I linger in the cramped kitchen of the Don Mills Achievement Center. Barb is director of the agency. Although just fifty, her hair is a lovely, untouched gray that sways in sensuous waves about her shoulders. She's a petite woman who effortlessly commands a room with a gentle voice and quiet manner. I can't remember how the topic arose, but we are talking about the Kennedy assassination, John that is. Barb was in first grade when it happened. I was a sophomore in college. In our relationship, I am supposed to be the wise, post-menopausal elder as Barb emerges into that exciting and confusing passage.

Barb has also recently become a grandmother through her partner Will. We share our states in life, marveling over their complexities, anxieties and joys. She talks about her new granddaughter, her daughter Sarah's engagement and a pending vacation in New England. I talk about my new grandson, Kai, Ian's September wedding and my recent vacation.

Three years after I joined the staff at Don Mills, I took time off so the family could renew our traditional summer visits to Stone Harbor, New Jersey. It was really Neely's idea. She wanted to introduce her husband and eventual children to the seaside village that held so many happy childhood memories for her. We packed up Mom, our friends, Jack and Elaine Baker, met up with Neel and Eric and settled into a spacious house on the bayside of the island.

One morning, on a solitary sunrise walk I watched two shrieking gulls scramble in the sand, playing tug-of-war with an unfortunate crab. They wrestled in a shallow tidal pool that ripples in the golden sunrise. Poor crab missed the last big wave to low tide. I found myself identifying with that unfortunate crustacean. I had an odd sense of being pulled both backward and forward, one wave short and stuck in the slack water.

Mom and Dad brought me to Stone Harbor for the first time in 1955. Mom was still adjusting to having only one child after Gigi's move to Edmonton. Dad tried to find a new and different sort of trip to catch her attention. I was an awe-filled twelve-year-old novice of the wonders of the place where the sea caresses the land. Engulfed in the salty air, sticky water and mesmerizing waves, I determined that this was where I wanted to be forever. How could we leave after just one week in paradise? How could we go back to a stifling, soot-laden Pittsburgh summer? On that sorrowful last night of our stay I pled my case.

"But why, Dad? You can get a job here. There's lots of houses to sell! They have schools and churches. Please, Dad."

Life can seem so uncomplicated to a twelve-year-old. Just sell the house and move. What's the big deal? Dad failed to grasp my pristine logic. He never gave in. So that first visit grew into a yearly trek, bringing friends, neighbors, my cute little cousin, Colleen, my new husband, our children, foster children, their friends and soon, a grandchild. How did all of those times and people come and go through my life so quickly? If it wasn't for the arthritic ache in my joints, I could almost have believed that I was still twelve. Well, twenty-two. Certainly no more than forty-two. But there I was at fifty-nine, waiting for the passage into yet another milestone decade in November.

Startled out of my self indulgent pondering by a shrill squawk, I watched gull number three enter the fray, crying the avian equivalent of "Mine! Mine! Mine!" Time to shake this mood and get on with my walk. No jogging on the beach this year, as month-old arthroscopic surgery on my left knee prohibited the pounding jar of anything beyond a fast walk. With an authoritative squawk, Mr. "Mine" Gull snatched the crab from the other two. That's what they get for making such a fuss. They could have quietly tugged it in half and had full tummies by then. Instead they stood facing out to sea, a slight breeze ruffling their feathers, watching as their would-be-breakfast was flown over the waves to the salt marshes where alpha gulls eat their lesser brethren's catch.

Time to stand and move on. When did I start having to think about the process of getting up? I used to just do it. Just had the desire to rise and my body complied.

With a soft grunt I stood up and resumed my walk on the damp, hard-packed sand. Back in our cottage my family and friends slept, unaware that a great shift was nudging my mental tectonic plates. I needed to stabilize them. I couldn't see it, hear it, smell it or explain it, but I felt an intense renewal, a beginning like no beginning I had ever before experienced, a beginning so mingled with an ending that the ingredients seemed inseparable. As I walked barefoot in the sand, sand that measured my way through early adolescence to adulthood, I sensed a new lane branching away from an old path.

The fat, little, baby feet of my children padded to the water on this sand. They held my fingers in their tight fists and squealed as the water rushed up over their thighs and diapered bottoms. How quickly soggy diapers were traded for tank suits and swimming trunks! Their hands then holding boogie boards and snorkels as they headed for depths beyond my comfort zone. Those chubby little feet are now the size fifteens of a successful, self-employed pharmacist, the sturdy Sauconys of a physical therapist and the sensible Rockports of a counseling psychologist.

It was so easy to allow a trickle of melancholy to seep through in this place. Alone under the huge sky, beside the raw power of the sea, I felt swallowed by a vastness that made me, and all I have done seem small and vulnerable. Fragmented reflections caught up in the moment and tumbled through my mind like the bits of shell and polished stone that rolled and rested, only to roll again in the rising tide. I felt hollow, as if the hidden moon pulled at my viscera along with the swelling waves. What was being washed away? What was sinking to the murky depths? What was left behind in the sand and sunshine of my life?

I turned to face the sun, by then floating several feet above the surface of the horizon and trudged back into the day. It was time to return to living my days, smiling, sharing, doing what was expected by those who didn't know about that shift onto a new path. The others would be waking soon. I strolled back through town, most of the shops empty, lingering in darkness for another few hours until the clerks would resuscitate them for the throngs of shoppers who would clog their aisles until well after the sun set. A teasing scent of baking bread lured me to the Bread and Cheese Cupboard, where I bought some warm sticky buns to go with the morning coffee my husband would be brewing by now.

Three years had receded since that pensive sunrise stroll on the Jersey shore when Terry and I returned to Stone Harbor to celebrate our fortieth anniversary.

We were married on June 24th 1967. We had summer jobs with the school district and postponed our honeymoon until August. I was so excited to share the island with my new husband, knowing that he too would fall in love with the quiet seaside town. We rented a little cottage beside Saint Paul's Catholic Church. It was a wonderful week of playing, relaxing and reveling in our passions. Terry loved the place. We sat side-by-side in the surf reading *In Cold Blood* and *The Death of a President.* We fished and crabbed in the bay and swam in the surf. By Friday morning we had a hefty catch of blue crabs. I planned my first gourmet dinner. We would have shrimp-stuffed flounder and fresh crab. Little did I imagine what would derail my romantic scheme.

In the cottages my parents had rented when I was a child, the kitchens were supplied with large aluminum cauldrons for boiling crabs. At the end of the day we returned from the beach and my mother filled the huge kettle with water, struggling with both hands on the handle to lift it to the burner. As we all showered and dressed for the evening, the water would slowly work its way up to a boil. Being a mountain dweller, it amazed me that water took so long to boil at sea level.

When the rest of the meal was prepared Mom dumped the crabs into the steaming maw of the pot where they boiled for six minutes, turning a dusty red.

Our tiny honeymoon cottage provided little more that an overgrown saucepan. Undaunted, I set the water to boil and at the appropriate time dumped the crabs in. Now when a crab hits boiling water it dies immediately causing a muscle to relax at the front of the shell, releasing a stream of air that unfortunately sounds like a tiny, crabby shriek. My beloved and, I was sure, heroic new husband shouted, "They're screaming!" and disappeared from the kitchen, leaving me to single-handedly catch five escapees skittering across the counters and floor.

As brides are remarkably resilient and forgiving, I pushed on with my culinary efforts. The flounder was light and perfectly done, the coleslaw just spicy enough, fresh rolls from the Bread and Cheese Cupboard wrapped in a warn towel rested on a fish-shaped cutting board, and, in the place of honor, a platter of artfully arranged red crabs, decorated with fresh parsley and lemon wedges. With an appreciative hug and kiss – those were the days when we couldn't keep our hands off each other – Terry sat at the table for two, glanced at the crabs, looked at me and said, "They still have eyes."

"That's how you serve crabs."

"They're looking at me!"

"They're dead."

"I know. I heard the screams."

He slid his plate of flounder and coleslaw to the edge of our little table, turned the crab-platter to face the wall and refused to try even one. Remarkably the union not only survived the honeymoon but also, as I said, has lasted forty years.

By the summer of our 2007 trip to Stone Harbor our vacationing group had grown far beyond the original snuggling, moon-eyed couple to a group of fourteen. These days I rent a two-story duplex, with a series of decks that open onto Shelter Haven Bay. Terry and I take a bay-front bedroom on the second floor. In the morning awaken to the brightening water glinting through a set of double windows. The water mirrors the houses that surround the bay, their classic seaside balconies, and weathered decks with boats resting motionless in the sheltered waters. Echoing caws of gulls sporadically burst into the dew-laden air, like the cachinnation of a group of old men sitting in a coffee shop, laughing at lewd jokes.

With no place to be at any particular time, I lie awake in bed and listen for the sounds of grandchildren stirring. I wait to greet the smiling girls then take my grandson Jake's hand and walk to Wawa, the Bread and Cheese Cupboard or Coffee Talk. Jake and I share mornings and evenings, our time alone to chat, eat donuts and fly kites.

The only family members missing this summer are Ian and Becky. They are too busy with their baby, Kai Kennevan, who was born the day before we left. However, we do have the Bakers, the kind of friends who have been with us so long and have been a part of so many family events through decades of deaths, births, weddings and holidays that the line between family and friendship has blurred to the point of erasure. Neel, Eric and the kids are joined this year by Rachel, Matt, Ken and Elisa, who flew up from Florida to be part of the family celebration. Ken Jones was a foster child who adopted us and has chosen to remain one of us. He lives in Fort Lauderdale with his bright, beautiful wife Elisa and year-old daughter, Mia Rose.

Ken came to us when he was fifteen years old and now, at 32, he strives to bring his young family into our fold. This holiday week provides the first opportunity since he has grown into manhood that Ken and I have had time and space for serious conversations. The night before he and his family return home we sit alone on the couch and talk on into the next morning. He reveals his feelings about the early days with the family, what it was like fitting in and dealing with the various personalities. He shares the turmoil of his troubled years when he left home for college and chose to stay away and "make it on my own, with no help."

On the beach I watch Mia toddling head-on into the rolling swells. Waves knock her to the sand, roll her over and before any adults can rush to her aid she staggers up with a spluttery smile, squinted eyes and totters back into the surf.

Mia Rose has the spunk to be a Kennevan woman, if not the genes. She shares the *something* her dad has that helped him fit in and weather the storms. Her mom, Elisa, the brave survivor of childhood leukemia, stirred her own hearty ingredients into the mix that is Mia Rose.

I thrive in this press of generations mingled in our two-story house. The rooms overflow with toys, beach paraphernalia, booster seats and geriatric walkers. Easy in their company as I travel along my new trail, I'm intrigued by memories of things I have lost and awareness of the things I have gained. I acknowledge what was transitory and what is permanent. I mourn what I took for granted, like time, my body and my mind. I recognize and accept things that thicken and harden and slow their functioning.

All of this is the grit I walk over on my new journey. It is a solid foundation for a new point of view. I no longer have a driving need to be liked, or to prove myself. I've done that. I know my strengths and recognize which limitations to accept. I trust, also, that there are challenges I can still face with a sputter and determined smile as I drive onward into the surge. My life steadily evolves into a mellow place where keen self-awareness slips brazen and independent from buried places.

Terry and I have a tennis match with the girls on the Friday morning of our vacation week. We are having a good time when I tease Terry about rationalizing a shot he missed. He does that a lot and it's a common friction between us. He gets mad, throws his racket on the ground and stomps off the court while I stand poised to serve. The fiery exchange that would have happened a decade ago fizzles in a wash of hurt and embarrassment that the girls have been part of the episode, and a sorrow that the last day was so tarnished. I harbored no hunger for the sharp retaliation that would have driven my retort half a decade ago. It's easier to let some things go now. Friends have died; children have been lost; the world has become a place of incomprehensible violence. What does a tennis game matter?

It's the physical changes that are most annoying and hardest to let go. I want to be beautiful again. I want to turn a head or two. A head more encouraging than the shriveled, gray-haired one belonging to an elderly man, wrapped head to toe in a white blanket, whom I encountered one afternoon on the beach at Ninety-third Street. As I passed by on the hot afternoon sand I greeted the dear old thing, propped in his folding lounge, with a smile and nod. He leered back lecherously and winked.

"Oh god!" I thought, "It's come to this," and trudged on, with quick steps across the burning sand, struggling to summon a stalwart determination to savor the spices that are left and never let life turn totally bland.

I splash into the crashing waves with my boogie board. I'm not the only gray-haired woman out here. As long as my knees get me past the breakers to wait for a perfect set, I'll be out here with the kids and a few brave elders. Funny though, while I bob, hanging off the edge of my red Morey board, watching the swell of incoming waves, judging the moment of break, I ponder being flipped and struck by a board, run over by someone and submerged. Are those low flying planes on shark watch? Did someone put sunscreen on the baby? I miss a great set lost in my daydream. The other riders skim and glide to shore. I'm left, a solitary swimmer obscured from land for the seconds that I slide down the back end of the swell.

Mom watches from her chair. Fortunately, she really can't see me this far away. It would make her nervous. She comes down to the beach now in a sand buggy loaned to her by the Stone Harbor Beach Patrol. It's a PVC pipe wheelchair perched on ballooning, pneumatic tires with a blue and white umbrella attached to the headrest. I can push her right into the lapping ripples. She squeals with each incoming wave that nudges the tires, bouncing the chair. No rider on a roller coaster enjoys more of a thrill. The outsized chair dwarfs her as Neely and Elisa set up pictures of mom holding Maddie and Mia on her lap.

The last night we bustle about bundling, cleaning and planning our morning departure. The kids are sleeping and most of the packing is done. I slip out of our apartment, walk barefoot down the steps and follow the route that Jake and I walked on our evening kite-flying expeditions. Approaching the beach, I smell the salty, clammy odor of low tide. I pass the fenced-in dunes and walk to the water's edge where the sand is packed hard by high tide and sit.

Darkness falls quickly, as the day's warmth seeps from the land into the cool night air. I stare across the blackened sea. Fleeting streaks of white foam mark each wave's break to the shore. The night sky, deserted by a new moon, is an open vault, blackened and differentiated from the water only by a sprinkling of stars. Once again I feel the weight of this passage into my sixties. This decade is my August.

When I was a kid and summer vacation began in June, the long days of summer seemed to stretch on forever. There were so many plans, so many things to do, places to go and people to hang out with. Mornings were lazy and easy. Nights were long, fresh adventures. Then the calendar on the kitchen wall flipped to August and a forlorn feeling of impending loss draped my days. September was in sight. Summer was a mortal thing with numbered days, days not to be squandered but treasured.

A similar lace of lonely melancholy fringes this sixth decade. I consider that when Mia and Maddie dress for their senior proms, I will be seventy-nine. When Jacob graduates I will be eighty. I may have two or three good decades left. I have a lot of living to stuff into those years, day by day, hour by hour. I draw the rich, salty, sulfury smell of the sea deeply into my lungs and savor the life-and-death flavor of it. I stand, still facing the receding tide, brush the damp grit from my shorts and turn with resolution.

On Saturday morning we all hug goodbye outside Uncle Bill's Pancake House and turn for home. Seven hours of road-time later we arrive. Ian and Becky bring Kai to Tidioute to welcome us home. We eat wings from the Landmark and pass the baby around, touching his tiny fingers and toes, smoothing his dark curly hair and watching his eyes that look too old and wise for such a tiny bundle. He's the last heir to Terry's branch of his family tree as his only brother had three daughters, and he carries the Kennevan name to another generation of William and Leah's line.

Edwards Brothers Malloy
Thorofare, NJ USA
April 22, 2013